Francis Bacon

Francis Bacon

Dawn Ades · Andrew Forge

with a note on technique by Andrew Durham
and a select bibliography

291 illustrations, 195 in colour,
including 21 fold-outs

Thames and Hudson
Published in association with The Tate Gallery

Frontispiece:
photograph of Francis Bacon by Jane Bown, 1980

Published on the occasion of the exhibition organized by
the Tate Gallery, 1985

Printed and bound in Great Britain by
Balding + Mansell Limited, Wisbech

CONTENTS

FOREWORD

It is a rare occurrence for a living artist to have two major retrospective exhibitions at the Tate Gallery. In the case of Francis Bacon, however, this should accord no surprise. Since his exhibition here in 1962 he has continued to produce work of outstanding quality, and we are honoured and delighted to be able to show again the paintings of this most distinguished artist.

His own work sets the standard for our time, for he is surely the greatest living painter; no artist in our century has presented the human predicament with such insight and feeling. The paintings have the inescapable mark of the present; I am tempted to add the word alas, but for Bacon the virtues of truth and honesty transcend the tasteful. They give to his paintings a terrible beauty that has placed them among the most memorable images in the entire history of art. And these paintings have a timeless quality that allows them to hang naturally in our museums beside those of Rembrandt and Van Gogh.

Bacon's painting challenges verbal explanation, and at the artist's request we have not provided the customary notes on each picture. We are, however, most grateful to Dawn Ades and to Andrew Forge for their illuminating essays, and to Andrew Durham of the Tate Gallery Conservation Department for his short piece on Bacon's technique. Krzysztof Cieszkowski, of the Tate Gallery library, has prepared a full bibliography, a shortened version of which appears here. This catalogue is a co-publication between the Tate Gallery and Thames and Hudson, and we would like to thank Thomas Neurath and Nikos Stangos in particular for their help in many ways.

We are very pleased to be able to show the exhibition in two of the greatest museums in West Germany after it leaves the Tate Gallery – at the Staatsgalerie, Stuttgart (October–December 1985) and at the Nationalgalerie, Berlin (February–April 1986). My colleagues, Dr Peter Beye and Professor Dr Dieter Honisch, have been most co-operative and helpful.

Richard Francis, Assistant Keeper at the Tate Gallery, has been responsible for the selection and presentation of the exhibition. He is greatly indebted to many people, among them David Sylvester, Valerie Beston, Thomas Gibson, and Anne Lutyens-Humfrey who prepared full listings of Bacon's works. Marlborough Fine Art have helped us at every stage in the preparation of the exhibition.

We are deeply grateful to the many private owners, in all parts of the world, who have generously let us borrow their paintings, and to the Directors and Trustees of almost thirty museums who have lent to us. Finally may I thank the artist himself. Such exhibitions as ours are often tedious, tiresome and disruptive to the artist who has better things to do. But we are most indebted to Francis Bacon for making this exhibition at the Tate Gallery possible and we know that our many visitors will wish to share our gratitude to him for the time and patience that he has devoted to us.

Alan Bowness
DIRECTOR

Dawn Ades

WEB OF IMAGES

Too much has been made of the 'horror' in Bacon's paintings both by critics and by the public. Bacon has always found this an irrelevant problem, denying that he ever intended to be 'horrific'. Yet he has, on the other hand, admitted that violence was central to his art, although the violence he is talking of only incidentally has anything to do with the 'horrific' in his work. When the disturbing and disquieting elements in his painting are discussed, it is usually in terms of subject matter, and a moral stance may be adopted towards his apparently grim imagery. 'I find the vision of man he uses his undeniable painterly talents to express quite odious', one critic recently wrote.[1] Others, still with the effect of making the paintings 'reflect' horror or violence in the world, describe it as mirroring the alienation and misery of mid-twentieth-century man. While, obviously, it is undeniable that Bacon has lived through and witnessed, in the common currency of our knowledge – films, news reports, photographs – the horrors of war, of concentration camps, and has experienced more directly the effects of violence in Ireland where he grew up, this does not mean that his painting is the mirror of this. Were it so, then John Berger's condemnation of his lack of indignation, such as Picasso expressed in *Guernica*, would indeed give grounds for disquiet.[2] Bacon makes the distinction between this 'mirrored' violence, and the mode in which he feels that violence enters his paintings, quite clear when answering David Sylvester's question about the 'distinct presence or threat of violence' conveyed in his work: 'This violence of my life, the violence which I've lived amongst, I think it's different to the violence in painting. When talking about the violence of paint, it's nothing to do with the violence of war. It's to do with an attempt to remake the violence of reality itself. And the violence of reality is not only the simple violence meant when you say that a rose or something is violent, but it's the violence also of the suggestions within the image itself which can only be conveyed through paint.'[3]

The main points here are, first, that violence in painting has nothing to do with illustrating violence; second, that the violence he is talking about can only be realized in a painted image; third, that it is not to do with the violent application of paint, with 'expressionist' violence, but comes out of 'suggestions within the image itself'.

Bacon has always been strongly opposed to painting as illustration, to painting which tells a story or becomes narrative. 'Illustrational form tells you through the intelligence immediately what the form is about, whereas a non-illustrational form works first upon sensation and then slowly leaks back into the fact.'[4] The opposition between intelligence and sensation is crucial for Bacon. Sensation may include intelligence but the intellect can bypass sensation. Bacon wants his painting to operate primarily through sensation, otherwise it becomes a mere vehicle: 'I want very, very much to do the thing that Valéry said – to give the sensation without the boredom of its conveyance. And the moment the story enters, the boredom comes upon you.'[5]

Bacon is very conscious of the peculiar conditions of painting today, which he describes as both very complicated and primitive, and which are partly a result of the advent of photography. 'As the thing's in such a terribly complicated stage now, the story that is already being told between one figure and another begins to cancel out the possibilities of what can be done with the paint on its own.' One problem is that the language in which we can talk of 'figurative' painting now has been impoverished, partly because of the simple opposition we are used to setting up between non-objective or abstract painting and figurative or representational painting. Bacon has seemed an isolated figure, his paintings set in a direction counter to most post-war art. Bacon considers abstract painting to be a wholly aesthetic thing, and any 'visceral' response we may claim to have to it is, he robustly asserts, just 'fashion'.[6] But this was not the only reason why he seemed to Andrew Forge to be, in the 1950s, violating 'every taboo that existed in English painting.' As Forge wrote, his paintings 'were concrete, worldly and grand and there was no precedent for them where everything from Ben Nicholson's abstract reliefs to Graham Sutherland's landscapes was in some sense or another romantic, ideal and intimately lyrical.'[7] There is no real precedent for the kind of tightrope walk he enacts between abstraction and figuration. The point is that he is trying to keep the 'recording' character of painting without slipping into illustration or story telling.

The elements of his painting can be isolated as follows: there is the material ground (the surface structure of the painting), there is the figure itself, and there is the setting or siting of the figure, more or less allusively established, and sometimes performing no more than a function of holding or isolating the figure. Sometimes the surface is painted with a single hue, sometimes areas of canvas (which he always uses reversed) are left naked. The variations of surfaces both within a single canvas and between different canvases is very striking. Two recent triptychs provide a good example: one, *Triptych, 1983* (123), is painted in vivid liquid pastel, a hue of orange-red unobtainable in oil paint, giving a rich, smooth surface. The other, *Three Studies for a Portrait of John Edwards*, 1984 (125), has a surface so light it is almost conjured out of air. The ground is divided, the upper part a very pale green-grey, the lower brown. The surface is dry, and as delicate as the portrait itself is tender, and in places it is powdered or lightly rubbed with paint. In earlier paintings in particular he would add sand to paint to manufacture a thick-textured surface, and occasionally the sand is heaped or clustered in certain areas to give a surface uneven in texture. At this point a further element should be mentioned: the glass behind which Bacon insists the painting should be placed as soon as it is finished. In a note to his gallery he explained that this was 'to give a unified texture to the painting without having to alter the abruptness of the technique in the painting . . . also to preserve the surface.'[8] The glass, then, is an essential element in the material surface of the paintings.

There is no illusion of real space for the figure to exist in; the body is isolated in its own localized space, which may be a chair or a bed, or may be just a frame of lines, sometimes visibly derived from the tubular 1930s furniture he himself used to make.

Since we so readily read a story into images, it is understandable that Bacon often deliberately destroys potential narrative or story content in his work, wilfully disrupts relationships between figures or between the figure and its setting. This is one reason for the predominance of the single figure in his canvases: once there are two or more figures the danger of the story 'talking louder than the paint'[9] becomes that much greater. It *is* possible to have several figures in a canvas without setting up a narrative, but under special conditions of figuration. Figures may, for example, be isolated from one another in the canvas, separated in their own, discontinuous spatial location. Another presence may be introduced through the device of a portrait within the painting, or by a reflection in a mirror – as in *Study of Nude with Figure in a Mirror*, 1969 (65) – and this reflection may not necessarily be that of the figure(s) in the canvas. Two figures may be so closely locked in physical embrace that their flesh is melded and dissolved, and their struggle becomes a single sensation – as in *Three Studies of Figures on Beds*, 1972 (78). Finally, there is the triptych itself, which both separates and links the figures within each panel.

The figure – and here I am not thinking so much of the portraits, though some of what I want to say of distortion and its origins also relates to the portraits – is first and foremost a body with a head. Often it has no face, and may be lacking part of its body or even its head. It is as though it is still in the process of realizing itself as a figure – it is not fully figurative. The French philosopher Gilles Deleuze suggests the term 'figural' to describe a process which both avoids abstraction and the illusionism of complete figuration.[10]

In the portraits and self portraits, where the face is necessarily important and cannot be ignored or destroyed in favour of the head alone (which is an appendage of the body rather than, like the face, a structure in its own right), Bacon uses rather different means of avoiding illustration.

There are several ways by which he 'destroys' appearance in order to remake a likeness. One is the use of non-rational marks, marks which have no obvious representational relationship with those areas of the face they are intended to depict. Bacon is obviously not the first painter

Illustration numbers in the text refer to the List of Works (p. 234), and also appear at the end of each caption in the plate section (p. 33).

to do this, and himself invokes the Rembrandt self portrait in Aix-en-Provence, in which 'there are hardly any sockets to the eyes . . ., it is almost completely anti-illustrational.'[11] The irrational marks may be a matter of chance: what was not accidental was Rembrandt's 'profound sensibility, which was able to hold onto one irrational mark rather than onto another.'

Bacon describes the involuntary marks that may begin the painting as a graph, and within this graph there are an enormous number of possibilities for 'planting facts' like the mouth or the eyes. 'Appearances are ambiguous', and endless in their possibilities: 'in a way you would love to be able in a portrait to make a Sahara of the appearance – to make it so like, yet having the distances of the Sahara.'[12] (This is reminiscent of the anxiety that gripped Giacometti when he contemplated the enormous distance that he felt when trying in a sculpture to cross from one side of the nose to the other.[13]) While in a painting of a 'figure' rather than a portrait the head may be so blurred as to have no features, in portraits the marks are often more specific. Sometimes, as I said, these may be irrational in terms of representation but nonetheless convey the fact of a nose or a mouth or a cheekbone. Sometimes Bacon may destroy one set of more or less precise marks with another – not blurring or smudging but painting *against*, as though to destroy a likeness perhaps of a photographic kind. In the 1964 *Study for Portrait (Isabel Rawsthorne)* (43), an almost photographic likeness is overlaid with streaky white or grey strokes which seem to delineate not just an alternative face but a different, nearly feline, head.

Distortion, fragmentation, isolation, then, are on one level the result of a pictorial battle against illustrative figuration, against a type of representation aimed solely at the intelligence. In his frequent uses of photographs – photography of almost any kind – the implications of these distortions can be seen as an attack on the too simple, too restricted, 'too ordered, too coherent' picture that photography 'gives of the interaction between man and his environment or one man and another',[14] or, indeed, of a single person.

Bacon's comments on the particular meaning of violence in his paintings quoted above continue directly into a consideration of problems posed by the portrait. 'When I look at you across the table,' he says to his interviewer David Sylvester, 'I don't only see you but I see a whole emanation which has to do with personality and everything else. And to put that over in a painting, as I would like to be able to do in a portrait, means that it would appear violent in paint. We nearly always live through screens – a screened existence. And I sometimes think, when people say my work looks violent, that I have from time to time been able to clear away one or two of the veils or screens.'

The clearing away of these screens or veils relates, as I hope to show, not only to the portraits. The point is that distortion is the result of an effort to convey a presence beyond likeness, to be able to bring into play a whole nexus of associations relating to that image, to convey the fact of a sensation as directly as possible: 'I'm just trying to make images as accurately off my nervous system as I can.'[15] As a materialist, Bacon deliberately says 'nervous system' rather than any more elevated or vague term like soul, or personality.

The distortions in his painting have sometimes been seen – rather lazily – as 'Expressionist'. But it is far from true to read them as a result of inflicting personal agitation or anguish onto people or objects so that they become deformed through frenzied or uncontrolled paint marks. Both chance and control are operating in Bacon in deliberate ways very different indeed from those of the Expressionists.

Bacon's figures, and not just those which are clearly engaged in action (usually sexual), but also those which are just standing or sitting, seem to be in the grip of a muscular force, a spasm of energy, which intensifies rather than diminishes their living presence. They are painted not as self-controlled, social creatures, but as beings driven by those urges or instincts Bacon describes as the irresistible counterpoint to the despair of contemplating death.

Bacon's seemingly violent and sometimes disquieting imagery has also been read as a direct result of a nihilistic attitude to life. The American writer Donald Kuspit, for instance, after describing the isolation of Bacon's figures 'sick with death – not necessarily literal death, but rather the feeling of being nothing', accounts for it as the result of a 'compulsive attention to the inevitability of death.'[16] Their loneliness, he suggests, communicates a 'general sense of oblivion' resulting from a deliberate cultivation of nihilism. 'Bacon, who has been called an existentialist . . . is simultaneously a decadent, in the sense of cultivating a nihilistic perception of and attitude to life.'

A different though still partial account of the isolation and distortion of Bacon's figures has been proposed above, which so far has not confronted the question of Bacon's 'nihilism', though it has suggested a strong response to physical presence. Bacon has made a number of comments about the futility or meaninglessness of life which have fed the view of him as nihilistic, but if they are considered more closely they are almost always carefully qualified: 'I think of life as meaningless; but we give it meaning during our own existence' . . . 'we are born and we die, but in between we give this purposeless existence a meaning by our drives.'[17]

The sense of futility is always countered by a profound exhilaration, springing not from any perverse obsession with 'death in life' or joy in death, but from life itself: 'I'm greedy for life; and I'm greedy as an artist. I'm greedy for what I hope chance can give me far beyond anything that I can calculate logically. And it's partly my greed that has made me what's called live by chance – greed for food, for drink, for being with the people one likes, for the excitement of things happening . . .'

The meaninglessness that Bacon takes for granted is that of life lived without belief in an after life, or in any moral absolutes. Many other systems of belief or codes of action, obviously, have been proposed to take the place of once dominant religious ideas, and the absence of these does not necessarily imply pessimism. Bacon is not particularly interested in subscribing to any other given set of beliefs, although he is profoundly interested in the philosophical problems involved. Like so many European artists of the earlier part of this century, he has been greatly attracted by Nietzsche, in particular by *The Birth of Tragedy* and *The Genealogy of Morals*. Nietzsche's passionate rejection of Christianity, in for example the later critical preface to *The Birth of Tragedy*, is expressed in terms of an affirmation of life with which Bacon would have much in common: 'From the very first, Christianity spelt life loathing itself, and that loathing was simply disguised, tricked out, with notions of an "other" and "better" life. A hatred of the "world", a curse on the affective urges, a fear of beauty and sensuality, a transcendence rigged up to slander mortal existence, a yearning for extinction, cessation of all effort until the great "sabbath of sabbaths" – this whole cluster of distortions, together with the intransigent Christian assertion that nothing counts except moral values, has always struck me as being the most dangerous, most sinister form the will to destruction can take . . .'[18]

Bacon may share something of Nietzsche's hypothesis of a 'strong pessimism',[19] but he phrases it for himself as a kind of internal dialectic: 'Ah well, you can be optimistic and totally without hope. One's basic nature is totally without hope, and yet one's nervous system is made out of optimistic stuff.' Deleuze formulated this as 'cerebrally pessimist, nervously optimist' (the original French *nerveusement* meaning 'of the nerves, sinews, sensations', rather than 'timidly').[20]

Since it has often been suggested that Bacon is in some sense an Existentialist, this should perhaps be looked at a little more closely. (Parallels have often been drawn between the claustrophobic windowless interior of Sartre's *Huis Clos* and the trapped space in Bacon's painting.) However, there is a real difference between his attitude to life and the stoic philosophy of Sartre, his 'stern optimism'.[21] In *L'Existentialisme est un humanisme*, Sartre defended Existentialism against the various charges made against it: that it led to the 'quietism of despair', that it emphasized human ignominy and the futility of the human enterprise, that it denied human solidarity by insisting on man's isolation. Sartre's answer to the Marxist and Catholic critiques – that by defining man in relation to his acts alone, rather than by any system of abstract values, he is affirming man's complete liberty, his moral freedom – stresses the optimism of Existentialism, and affirms it as a humanism. This is couched, in a sense, too much in terms of man's moral dilemma as a social being to appeal to Bacon. For Bacon any answer lies not in a harsh or dogged optimism, but in the tension between 'cerebral pessimism' and 'nervous optimism'.

In considering Bacon in relation to Existentialism, connections are necessarily of a tenuous kind, given that it was primarily a theoretical and literary movement. With Surrealism, however, with which, again, Bacon has been associated, more specifically visual connections have been drawn. Bacon himself is more interested in Surrealist ideas and in Surrealist poetry than in Surrealist painting, and it is perhaps only in the apparent incongruity of the imagery of *Painting 1946* (5) that something like Surrealist juxtaposition has been allowed to stand. The transformation involved in the genesis of this painting has also been seen as bearing witness to an early disposition towards Surrealism: 'I was attempting to make a bird alighting on a field. And it may have been bound up in some way with the three forms that had gone before, but suddenly the lines that I'd drawn suggested something totally different, and out of this suggestion arose this picture.'[22] It is clear, then, that if this painting is to be associated at all with Surrealism, it is in the process of transformation through accident and suggestion.

Bacon's use of accident and chance, his natural acceptance of the transforming and motivating powers of the unconscious, can in a sense be related to Surrealism, but they do not come out as a commitment to the Surrealists' ideas and beliefs in any systematic way. His use of chance marks, and of accident, has a different genesis and is subject to different procedures from Surrealist automatism or from Duchamp's controlled philosophical experiments with chance. While the Surrealists aimed to 'trap' images from the unconscious through automatic drawing, or in the unwilled figurations thrown up by techniques like *frottage*, images which could have the character of revelation and of the marvellous about them, Bacon is not interested in quarrying the unconscious in this sense. He may at any point in a painting make random paint marks – throwing, scrubbing or sponging the paint (or all three), sometimes to break a spell when the painting is not going well, or to destroy the conventional, the pictorial cliché ('half my painting activity is disrupting what I can do with ease').[23] In some ways this is only to intensify the already unpredictable behaviour of the fluid medium of paint. He may at the last minute add a streak or dash of randomly splashed paint – then either leave it or not. It is not a matter of accepting unquestioningly what chance or the unconscious throws up and valuing it then for its own sake. If the random marks work, it is because they have a 'kind of inevitability' about them, and the result in the end is a balance between immediacy and control.

Bacon is not interested either, by contrast with the Surrealists, in the potential of symbolism, in the kind of visual paraphrase of dream processes after Freud that were created by Ernst or Dalí. He is interested rather in things themselves, enriched as they may be by associations, or in facts that he is attempting to trap: 'Now I feel that I want to do very, very specific objects, though made out of something which is completely irrational from the point of view of being an illustration.'[24]

Bacon's position vis-à-vis Surrealism is clarified if it is approached from what may seem to be a tangential comparison: with Georges Bataille, who once described himself as Surrealism's 'old enemy from within'. Bacon shares a number of Bataille's preoccupations, during above all a specific period when Bataille was engaged in a polemic with Surrealism; while, that is, he was editing and writing in the magazine *Documents* between 1929 and 1930. *Documents* was the refuge for several disaffected Surrealist writers and painters, including Michel Leiris, a long-standing friend of Bacon's, who has also written on him and whose portrait Bacon has painted, as well as Miró and Giacometti.[25] A number of Bataille's texts in *Documents* can be read as implicit attacks on Surrealism, particularly on what Bataille felt was an evasive and poetic idealism in Surrealism which conflicted with its stated commitment to dialectical materialism. Breton counter-attacked in his *Second Manifesto of Surrealism*, and the terms in which he castigates Bataille are not dissimilar to those used by some critics against Bacon: 'M. Bataille professes that he only wants to consider the vilest, most discouraging and corrupted things in this world . . .'[26]

Bacon possessed copies of *Documents*, and has talked specifically about the effect some of the illustrations reproduced in them had upon him, notably those of slaughterhouses, which will be discussed below. It was not just the illustrations, however, but the whole context of ideas in which these illustrations were situated, that must have touched Bacon. To clarify the implications of this, I want to take a specific image which obsessed Bacon almost from the start of his painting career: the mouth.

Stretched in a grimace or a cry, or even perhaps in a smile, the mouth was often the most prominent or even the only feature in some of the earliest of Bacon's heads and figures. Some of Bacon's direct sources for the human cry have been identified by a number of critics – the wounded, screaming nursemaid from the Odessa steps sequence of Eisenstein's *Battleship Potemkin* (p. 15), the desperate mother in Poussin's *Massacre of the Innocents*, perhaps too Caravaggio's *Medusa*. He has also spoken of his fascination with a 'second-hand book which had beautiful hand-coloured plates of diseases of the mouth, beautiful plates of the mouth open and of the examination of the inside of the mouth, and they fascinated me, and I was obsessed with them.'[27] Later, he thought his screams were too abstract, thay they might have been more successful had they 'been more conscious of the horror that produced the scream.'[28] But Bacon's avoidance of the direct products of horror has already been explained in the context of his determined avoidance of a kind of figurative painting which could slide into illustration. The photographs and texts in *Documents* could have been a source in that one of their main characteristics was that of presenting a material sensation as directly as possible, and in the process stripping away some of the veils or screens, some of the hypocrisies, with which we try to conceal and make palatable bald existence.

One of the photographs by another ex-Surrealist, J.-A. Boiffard, reproduced in *Documents*, was of an open, screaming mouth, and it accompanied a short text by Bataille, one of his 'critical dictionary' entries on 'La Bouche' ('The Mouth').[29] This focuses on the fact that it is through the mouth that our most concentrated experiences of agony or ecstasy are physiologically expressed, and also that in this expression the human draws particularly close to the animal. Bataille wrote: 'On great occasions human life is concentrated bestially in the mouth, anger makes one clench one's teeth, terror and atrocious suffering make the mouth the organ of tearing cries. It's easy to observe on this subject that the stricken individual, in stretching out his neck, frantically lifts up his head, so that the mouth comes to be placed, so far as is possible, in the extension of the vertebral column, that is to say in the position it normally occupies in the animal constitution.'

It is possible to trace in Bacon's early images concentrating on or significantly including the mouth, several characteristics which run parallel with Bataille's text: first, the presence of the mouth alone among the features of a figure; second, the peculiar animal-extension of the neck instanced by Bataille; and third, a more general and deliberate dwelling upon the shared characteristics of man and animal.

The cry shares the character of the laugh in that it is, as Julia Kristeva says when writing about Bataille, both 'evaporation of meaning and the only possibility of communication.'[30] Speech may be the sign of human intelligence, eyes the window to the soul, but the cry, visibly speechless, is an instinctive spasm of the body. The figures of the Eumenides, in Bacon's 1944 triptych, *Three Studies for Figures at the Base of a Crucifixion* (1), have no eyes, but only mouths. The creature in the centre panel, which resembles a huge flightless bird rather than a human, has its eyes bandaged. In that on the right, the upper part of the face is lacking, an absence accompanied by or produced by another severe distortion: the neck is abnormally prolonged, ending in a savage jaws/mouth. This is suspended horizontally like an animal snout, though the rest of the body is vestigially, in spite of its posture, closer to that of a human. The bird-animal aspect of the Eumenides, the Furies who pursued the matricide Orestes in the final part of the *Oresteia* of Aeschylus, is implicit in the broken and ambiguous description of them:

> an amazing company –
> women, sleeping, nestling against the benches . . .
> not women, no,
> Gorgons I'd call them; but then with Gorgons
> you'd see the grim, inhuman . . .
> I saw a picture
> years ago, the creatures tearing the feast
> away from Phineus –
> *These* have no wings,
> I looked.[31]

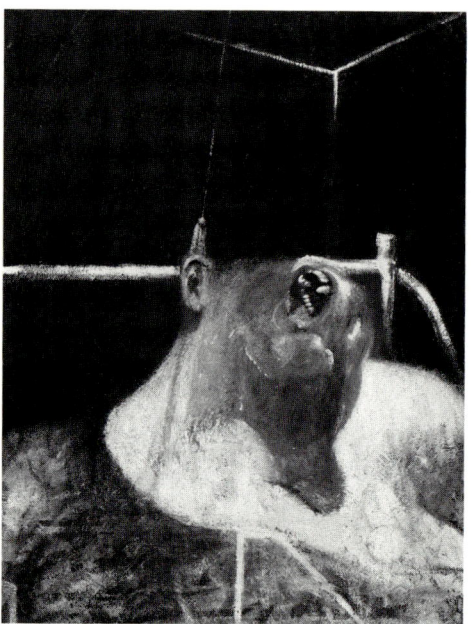

Head I, 1948

Head II, 1949

In a series of heads of the late 1940s, the cry effects the same anatomical distortion, though now the subject is clearly human. In *Head I* of 1948 the mouth is tilted sideways as though to emphasize the spinal extension Bataille describes, the neck and cheek bulging massively as though attempting to contain and suppress the bestial spasm. It is possible to read into the neck at the right a configuration which is not just bulging flesh but a second neck culminating in the mouth, which itself thereby becomes, as in the right-hand panel of the earlier triptych, the substitute for the complete head. When painting this head, Bacon was looking at a photograph of a chimpanzee, and it is clear that the extended canine teeth are animal, not human. This is true also of *Head II* (1949). In *Head IV* (1949) the chimpanzee or monkey appears on the man's shoulder.[32] When Bacon painted the chimpanzee itself, in 1955 (29), it had the same mouth, with the head also tilted sideways and up, for the chimpanzee shares most of its anatomy with man, and therefore would, ironically, share the same distorting extension to achieve expression of the cry.

Bacon's man/animal imagery could now be brought back to Bataille's treatment of this theme. In the first sentence of the passage quoted above Bataille brought into direct rapport 'great human occasions' and 'bestially', and as the passage goes on is clearly challenging the value normally placed on the terms 'human' and 'animal'. This might be clarified if we look at another characteristic set of themes: noble/ignoble/base. Bataille distends or subverts the usual value accorded the term 'base', in the paradigm noble/base, and may use it either in a positive and laudatory way, as for example in the title of one of the *Documents* texts, 'Le Bas Matérialisme et la gnose', or negatively, but in a context in which this negation itself is shocking: 'l'orientation bassement idéaliste du Surréalisme' ('the basely idealistic direction of Surrealism'). The violent pulling together of man/beast in such a way that the traditional distinction between them is brought into question was part of Bataille's continual attack on the 'idealist deception' that man practises upon himself. In this case it involves the revelation of the animal or near-animal in man in those situations above all when he believes himself to be at his most human or noble. A comparable idea could be at work in Bacon. Deleuze suggests that the animal traits of certain figures and heads in Bacon involves a double significance: man becomes animal, but not without the animal taking on something of the *esprit* of man. There is, in other words, a zone of non-discrimination between man and animal. But this is not to be seen as a 'lowering' of man to the level of beast.

Bacon has said that the *Head* of 1948 was in fact a woman – was it perhaps then thematically related to the Eumenides? The upper part of the head is engulfed in black, so that all attention is

Head III, 1949

Head IV, 1949

focused on the mouth. It is not a question of the dehumanizing of the human figure, but of giving the animal characteristics of a human in a moment of extreme experience.

Head III, in the 1949 series, is a striking reversal of the two earlier heads: the mouth is gripped tight shut, and everything is concentrated in the piercing gaze, vivid black pupils framed in the pince-nez, which echoes that of the stricken nursemaid in *Battleship Potemkin*. The difference between this and the earlier heads, the physical contrast, is again illuminated by Bataille in 'La Bouche': 'This . . . puts into relief the importance of the mouth in physiology or even in animal psychology, and the general importance of the upper or lower extremity of the body, orifice of profound physical impulses: one sees at the same time that a man can liberate these impulses in at least two different ways, in the brain, or in the mouth, but the moment the impulses become violent he is obliged to turn to the bestial manner to liberate them. Whence comes the narrowly constipated character of a strictly human attitude, the magisterial aspect of the face with its mouth closed, beautiful as a strong-box.'

This in a sense completes the argument, for it is not that man in his scream sinks to the level of animal, but that this animal element is necessary and a part of him, and without it he is restricted or 'constipated'.

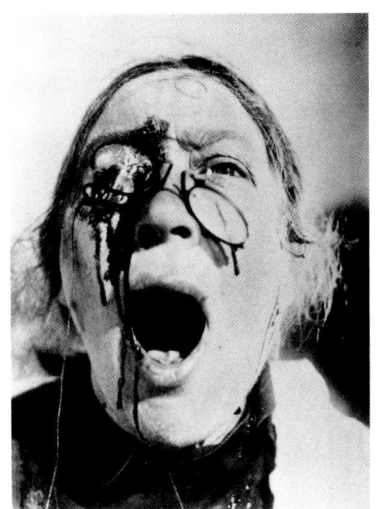

Eisenstein, still from *Battleship Potemkin*, 1925

When Bacon painted his versions of Velasquez's *Pope Innocent X*, immediately after the *Heads* discussed above, several works similarly have mouths stretched wide in a cry: *Study after Velasquez*, 1950, for example, or *Pope I* and *Pope II*, 1951 (12, 13). Perhaps his idea was to test one of the greatest portraits ever painted, of a man set highest above his fellow men (the archetypal father, verging on the divine) in the grip of a feeling so intense that the only expression of it brought him close to the beasts.

It must be emphasized that it is not the intention here to suggest that Bacon was in any sense illustrating Bataille, but rather that their concerns, preoccupations and attitudes run parallel.

Bacon's obsession with the image of the mouth moves also in other directions. To a certain extent it is concerned with a purely visual response to the mouth irrespective of its human construction in either cry or laugh. He has spoken of liking the 'glitter and colour that comes from the mouth, and I've always hoped in a sense to be able to paint the mouth like Monet painted a sunset.'[33] Being thoroughly aware of Freudian ideas, he is also probably aware of an explicit sexual symbolism connected with the mouth: 'I've always been very moved by the movement of the mouth and the teeth. People say that these have all sorts of sexual implications, and I was always very obsessed by the actual appearance of the mouth and teeth, and perhaps I have lost that obsession now, but it was a very strong thing at one time.'[34]

Studies from the Human Body, 1975

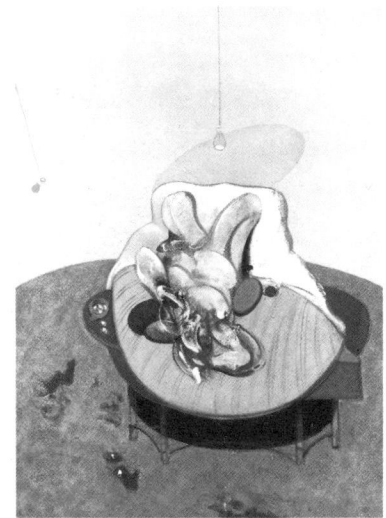

Lying Figure, 1969

It is a commonplace of Freudian theory that sexual repression as it is manifested, for example, in dreams, frequently 'makes use of transpositions from a lower to an upper part of the body.'[35] Bacon is certainly not making any deliberate call on psychoanalysis, in which he does not have much interest; there are no direct transpositions of one part of the body to another in any selfconscious or systematic way, and indeed he expresses a definite scepticism about the whole problem of interpretation of this kind. Talking of the problem of explaining what chance is and how it operates, he said 'I don't think one can explain it. It would be like trying to explain the unconscious. It's also always hopeless talking about painting . . .'

Nonetheless, there are certain pictorial means by which a particular image is invested with a sexual potency of a special kind, and one which quite often involves the mouth/teeth/head. There is, for example, a curious kind of inversion in certain paintings of nude figures on a bed, in which the nude is turned so that the head is towards the lower edge of the picture frame, the legs and genitals to the upper edge: *Studies from the Human Body* of 1975, for example, or *Lying Figure* of 1969, or *Lying Figure with Hypodermic Syringe* of 1963 (40). In the latter two, the facial features and the genital areas are so indistinct as to blur any notion of gender or specific personality, but in the *Studies from the Human Body* teeth and sex are distinct. Although the mouth/teeth/head are in the correct position, there is nonetheless a concentration of sexual energy and aggression in them that seems partly to spring from their inverted positions. In another figure, the lowest in *Three Figures and a Portrait*, 1975, the body itself is so vague, its physical components so fluidly defined, that the mouth/teeth are the only clear feature, but their relation to the other parts of the body – whether, in other words, they are located in the head or the genitals – is impossible to determine.

One further comparison in connection with the motif of the mouth could be made between specific figures in two paintings: the figure in the central panel of the *Oresteia* triptych of 1981, and the left-hand figure in *Three Figures and a Portrait*. The relationship between the head and the body is similar, defined by the strongly marked vertebrae which, in the *Oresteia* figure, also form a neck. The humped shoulders, incidentally, from which the vertebrae sweep down, trace back to a 1944–5 painting, *Study for a Figure*, one of those that immediately followed the Eumenides triptych, and reappear recently (anatomically vague, sexually suggestive and figurally potent) in the nude figures with cricket pads (113). The figure in *Three Figures and a Portrait* has an unusually complete head (such heads are more common in recent paintings), and is a posthumous portrait of Bacon's close friend George Dyer. This is singled out from the rest of the body by the use of the radiographer's 'target' circle.[36] This circle, drawn round the part of the body to be photographed in medical guides to aid the correct positioning of bodies for

Three Figures and a Portrait, 1975

Illustration from K.C. Clark, *Positioning in Radiography*, 1939

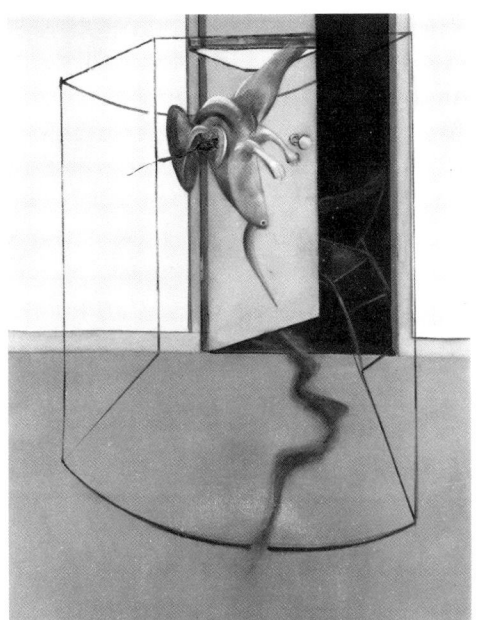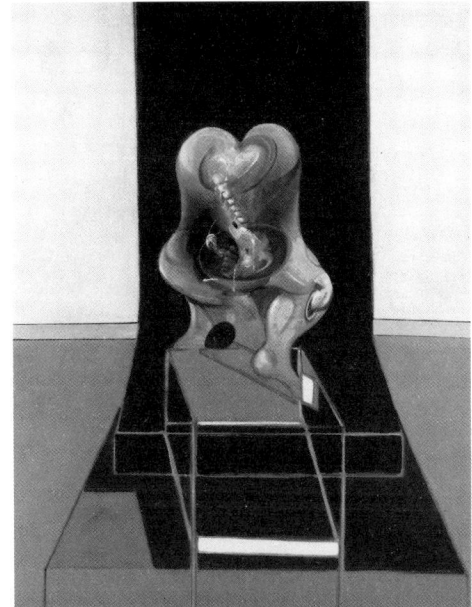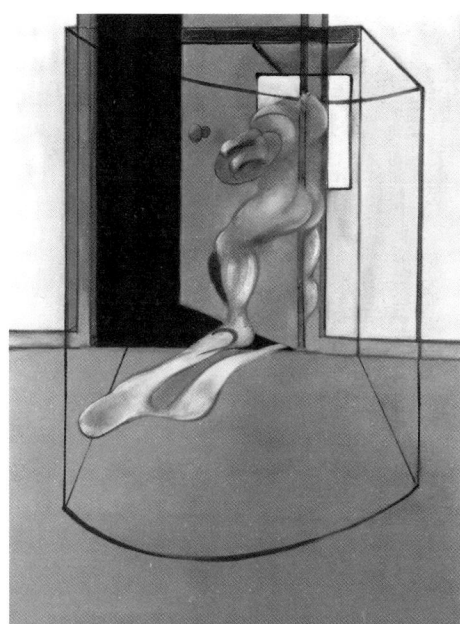

Triptych Inspired by the Oresteia of Aeschylus, 1981

radiography, is used here to demarcate a change of focus in the painting, although this change is not consistent. The beige ground of the room-space darkens and changes in texture, as though suddenly magnified through a strong lens; the head, though, does not change in scale in relation to the rest of the body, nor is it made transparent as though in an x-ray. It is, however, clearly defined in feature both in relation to its own body and to the other figures in the room, including the portrait. In keeping with this, the figure starts off neatly dressed, in the area defined by the circle, with a white collar, but outside the circle the figure is naked, the backbone clearly visible, as though the x-ray is operating perversely in the area *outside* the circle. When, as we tend to do by analogy with the top right-hand figure whose circled area is clearly magnified, we try to read Dyer's head as *closer* to us, we are immediately confronted by a sharp white splash of paint, manifestly on the surface of the painting, unresolvable as anything but a splash of paint and yet also a disrespectful substitute for the tie that should have been there, which pierces the circle and pins the head back into submission to the body. In the central figure of the *Oresteia* triptych, the head is also swept downwards on an extended neck and placed in what is now clearly a genital position, teeth glowing in hollowed flesh set in a dark circle, a dab of cloudy white paint dribbling from between them. So the 'displacement' of mouth or teeth to the genital area, and a condensation there of sexual energy, is accomplished without gratuitous or wholly irrational distortion.

Study for a Figure, 1944–5

There is one final 'charge' or association possessed by the mouth for Bacon, which rises from the fact that this orifice is the most prominent visible opening in the head and the body. Bacon said 'one could make a mouth in a way – I mean it comes about sometimes, one doesn't know how – I mean you could draw the mouth right across the face as though it was almost like the opening of the whole head, and yet it could be like the mouth. . .'[37] In the *Seated Figure* of 1979 the mouth stretches across the whole width of the jaw, almost like the teeth/jaws of a skull, revealed by x-ray if we imagine the head seen frontally, but if read as a profile head in line with the black shadow profile it is as though the mouth stretches right across the head. This emphasizes the mouth in relation to the head as bodily organ, not the mouth as one of a set of features defining an individual personality. But the sense of 'opening' goes further than this, for the mouth itself can also be metaphor for a wound. A line from the *Oresteia* which has haunted Bacon for some time is that spoken by the leader of the Furies, or the Eumenides, as they track Orestes to Athena's sanctuary: 'the reek of human blood smiles out at me'.[38]

This line shocks because of the clashing of disgust ('reek') and joy ('smiles'), but more because of the extraordinary synaesthesia of the metaphor: the wound gapes in the flesh like a smile in the face, but the blood is present not just visually but through the sense of smell. It is

Seated Figure, 1979

this kind of image, its knotted complex of associations which appeal to a totality of bodily sensation, that obsesses Bacon in poetry, and above all in Aeschylus. A very early painting by Bacon exhibited in 1934, and which he regretted destroying, was *Wound for a Crucifixion* – a painting of a specimen wound mounted on a sculptor's armature, against the wall of a hospital corridor or ward. A more recent painting of a wound occurs in the left-hand panel of *Triptych – Studies of the Human Body*, 1979 (107), a red streak in a painting otherwise remarkably hygienic and athletic. Bacon does not make any direct metaphoric or symbolic use of the wound/mouth images, but in many images appeals in some way, however distant, to a nexus of associations they may share as openings in the body.

Rembrandt, *Slaughtered Ox*, 1655. Oil on panel. The Louvre, Paris

Among the photographs in *Documents* are two from a series taken by Eli Lotar when he accompanied the painter André Masson to the slaughterhouses at La Villette. Masson was about to do a series of works based on the theme of massacres; in 1937 he illustrated Bataille's text *Sacrifices* with five etchings representing Mithra, Orpheus, the Sacrificed, the Minotaur and Osiris. Other ink drawings he made for Bataille's review *Acéphale* represent the headless man, the Minotaur and scenes of cosmic and dionysian sacrifice.

The photographs by Lotar were reproduced to accompany another of Bataille's critical dictionary entries, 'Abattoir' ('Slaughterhouse'). Slaughter and sacrifice were, Bataille argued, once linked; they were aspects of the same act and happening in one place: 'The slaughterhouse rises out of religion in the sense that the temple of distant epochs served a double function, being used at the same time for supplication and for killings. From this resulted a disturbing coincidence between mythological mysteries and the lugubrious grandeur of places where blood flows.'[39] The real thrust of the text, however, is not really towards a dubious nostalgia, but towards an exposure of the insipid, blinkered, hypocritical and hygienic life of modern man. The 'quarantine' that hides abattoirs from our sight is a sign of our inability, in Bataille's view, to tolerate our own ugliness.

There are enough points of comparison on this subject between Bataille and Bacon to warrant closer examination. A recurrent subject of Bacon's from the 1930s has, of course, been the Crucifixion. One *Crucifixion*, showing the strong influence of Picasso, who also probably guided him in the choice of subject, was the first work by Bacon to be reproduced (in Herbert Read's *Art Now*, of 1933). Although painted over ten years before the point at which Bacon considers his serious painting career to have begun, with *Three Studies for Figures at the Base of a Crucifixion* of 1944, this *Crucifixion* already shares some of the preoccupations of later paintings. The figure (its reduced stick-like forms harking back to Picasso) is isolated against a dark ground, and there appear to be lines or markers of space round it, besides the dark form of the Cross itself, which anchor it to the edges of the canvas without providing any kind of 'illusionistic' space. Most striking, though, is the light-coloured form sweeping out around the body of the figure, almost like a second figure or the aura of another figure. At the lower end of the figure to the right, there are three broad strokes, parallel and oriented at an angle which must suggest a rib cage, though whether that of emaciated human or carcass would be impossible to say. In *Painting 1946* (5) such a conjunction is again suggested. The huge carcass framing the grinning demagogue is hung in such a way that it clearly evokes a Crucifixion. Bacon was not the first artist to bring into play, however distantly, this connection. The strange dignity of Rembrandt's carcass of beef, and the intensity of Goya's, both suggest distant associations with each artist's treatment of the Crucifixion. Bacon, in his 1933 *Crucifixion*, like Picasso, empties the theme of any religious significance, but does not appear to put the same emphasis on the pain, anguish and horror of the event. In *Three Studies for a Crucifixion*, 1962 (39), and in the central panel of the *Crucifixion* triptych of 1965 (45), the man/flesh/carcass theme is quite ambiguous. The figural form as a whole was prompted by the Cimabue *Crucifixion*, which Bacon says he always thought of 'as an image – as a worm crawling down the cross'. In the right-hand panel of *Three Studies of a Crucifixion*, the flesh and the rib cage make the carcass explicit. The undulating slabs of flesh in the central panel of the 1965 triptych are less obviously animal carcass, but Bacon has added here two rigid limbs, encased in plaster splints, but ending in the kind of formless knobs of a flayed carcass. Bacon in

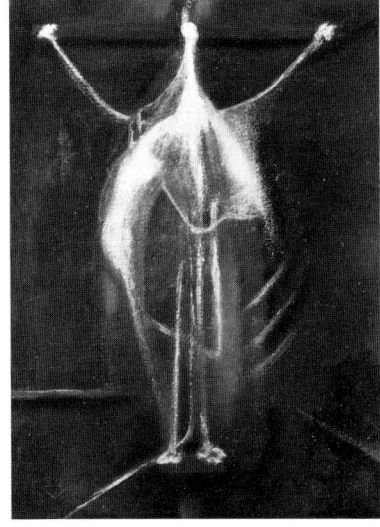

Crucifixion, 1933

his paintings makes an explicit connection between the Crucifixion and the abattoir, which has certain things in common with Bataille.

When Bacon was asked why he chose the theme of the Crucifixion for the 1962 triptych (39), he replied as follows: 'I've always been very moved by pictures about slaughterhouses and meat, and to me they belong very much to the whole thing of the Crucifixion. There've been extraordinary photographs which have been done of animals just being taken up before they were slaughtered; and the smell of death. We don't know, of course, but it appears by these photographs that they're so aware of what is going to happen to them, they do everything to attempt to escape. I think these pictures were very much based on that kind of thing, which to me is very, very near this whole thing of the Crucifixion. I know, for religious people, for Christians, the Crucifixion has a totally different significance. But as a non-believer, it was just an act of man's behaviour, a way of behaviour to another.'[40]

There is, running through this, the idea already discussed that there is a 'zone of non-discrimination' between man and animal – and even the thought, in the passage above, that the animal's awareness depends on senses that we may have lost. It is possible that the figures in the 1944 triptych are also animals lifting their heads as they sense death and their own fate.

Bacon also shares with Bataille to a certain extent the idea that the grand sites of religious sacrifice cannot be separated from the slaughterhouses, though this is not intended to suggest that he shares Bataille's ritual/sacramental idea that man *needs* sacrifice. He does, however, share Bataille's revulsion against the hypocrisy of averting one's eyes from the slaughterhouses: 'When you go into a butcher's shop and see how beautiful meat can be and then you think about it, you can think of the whole horror of life – of one thing living off another. It's like all those stupid things that are said about bull-fighting. Because people will eat meat and then complain about bull-fighting covered with furs and with birds in their hair.'[41]

Many artists and writers have over the last hundred years gone back to the image of the Crucifixion but for reasons that are extra-religious and in a non-Christian context. It has been used to express spiritual or transcendental attitudes, or, as in the case of Picasso, pain or anguish. Bacon talks of it as an 'armature' on which to hang 'feelings about behaviour and the way life is'. These feelings are very private, and involve a whole nexus of associations and sensations, and Bacon even suggests that painting the Crucifixion is akin to painting a self portrait.

The Greek myths are more distant from us even than the Crucifixion, but are brought closer to us again through the writings of those like Nietzsche and Freud, who used them to validate their own ideas about man in his aesthetic and psychic relation to life. Freud hung a theory central to psychoanalysis on the myth of Oedipus, whose actions in killing his father and marrying his mother were, in Freud's opinion, expressive of a universal impulse, one of the 'primeval wishes of our childhood'. In Jung's view, one of Freud's great services to mankind was the rescuing of Greek mythology from the dusty recesses of literary history. Nietzsche in *The Birth of Tragedy* 'claimed that art, rather than ethics, constituted the essential metaphysical activity of man,'[42] and analysed the development of Greek tragedy in terms of the opposing Dionysian and Apollonian forces in art.

Bacon has referred to Greek tragedy at least since the 1944 triptych, where he brought it into direct relation to the Crucifixion by describing the figures at the base of the cross as Eumenides. He is referring already to the tragic myth of Orestes, who killed his mother Clytemnestra in revenge for her murder of his father Agamemnon, and as a result was pursued by the Eumenides whose function was the punishment of 'incestuous' murder. It is significant that he, like Bataille, preferred this to the Oedipus tragedy. This is attributable not just to his response to the myth itself but to his preference for Aeschylus over Sophocles or Euripides. A book that he has valued for a long time is a study of the literary rediscovery of Aeschylus, by W.B. Stanford, *Aeschylus in his Style: A Study in Language and Personality*, which was published in Dublin in 1942. Stanford argues that, although Aeschylus was much respected in theory as the founder of Greek tragedy, his 'rough, bold poetics' were relegated in favour of the polished perfection of Sophocles from the time of Sophocles himself until the nineteenth century. Aeschylus' imagery offended against the classical ideal of lucidity, coherence and rationality, and the rediscovery of his work only began with Romanticism. Stanford's account of

Aeschylus provides considerable insight into both Bacon's imagery and his concept of conveying the 'facts' of sensations. Aeschylus' obscurity, Stanford points out, is the result of the expression of 'half-formed thoughts', which are in fact skilful ways of conveying the inarticulacy or incoherence caused by extreme emotion. His imagery is violent to express the inner effects of emotion: fear makes the heart turn black and vibrate, 'these inner sensations of tossing, tearing, darkening, raving, burning, freezing, prophesying, oozing, came from his own passionate heart.' Aeschylus was the Dionysian in Nietzsche's sense, and Stanford also proposes a parallel with the obscurity of twentieth-century poets, who have themselves, like T.S. Eliot, rediscovered Aeschylus. Stanford describes Aeschylus as trying to express the participation of all the senses, as in the line 'the reek of blood smiles out at me.' He tended to prefer metaphor to simile: 'metaphor is a concentrating intensive figure, congenial to a mind that seizes broad analogies without pausing to reflect on accompanying dissimilarities of detail', and relies far less than Sophocles or Euripides on synecdoche or metonymy, types of imagery which, in Stanford's opinion, show a desire for variety rather than imagination. He favours synaesthetic imagery, and sustained and mixed metaphor. He was capable of shocking travesties of conventional simile, as in his treatment of the spring/birth simile in the following passage. Clytemnestra, rejoicing over the dead body of Agamemnon, whom she has just drawn to his death over the blood-red tapestries, says:

> And squirting out a sharp death-gush of blood,
> He strikes me with dark drizzle of murderous dew,
> And I rejoiced as the sown corn-fields rejoice
> At the god-sent glistering when the buds are born.

This, Stanford observes, is 'as dark a piece of literary blasphemy as has ever been uttered.'

Bacon painted his 1981 triptych while reading the *Oresteia*, and it has been given the title *Triptych Inspired by the Oresteia of Aeschylus*. The three images cannot, nor should we expect them to, be located in any specific scene from the *Oresteia*. Nor can each separate painting be linked serially in a dramatic progression following the three-part structure of the trilogy, although the trilogy form of classical Greek tragedy may have confirmed Bacon in his preference for the triptych.

Painting, obviously, obeys different laws from those of drama, and it is natural that what would be a climax in drama, occurring at or near the end of an act should in a triptych be placed in a central panel, just as the Crucifixion is placed centrally in an altar piece. Bacon by no means always invests a central panel of a triptych with any greater or climactic value than the other panels, but in the 1981 triptych the central panel is dominant. The whole image conveys the 'lugubrious grandeur of places where blood flows', and, although the central figure cannot be specifically identified, the whole image seems to refer to the first part of the *Oresteia*, *Agamemnon*. It condenses the scenes where Agamemnon, victorious in the Trojan War, is welcomed home by Clytemnestra, who leads him into the palace and murders him in revenge for the sacrifice of their daughter Iphigenia at the start of the War. Clytemnestra and her women have spread dark red tapestries before Agamemnon, which Aeschylus describes in a characteristic metaphor of blood:

> Let the red stream flow and bear him home
> To the house he never hoped to see – Justice
> lead him in . . .

The carpet flows and is the colour of blood, home is both the palace, and the death which awaits him within. The great slab of dark crimson paint, both carpet and royal dais, surrounding and raising the figure, is the same colour as the blood that trickles under the door in the left-hand panel. Both Agamemnon, and at the end of the second part of the trilogy, *The Libation Bearers*, Clytemnestra, are murdered offstage, though the bodies of each are revealed at the end. The presence of the curious bird creature in the left-hand panel suggests one of the Furies, who appear only after Orestes has killed Clytemnestra.

Each image in the triptych condenses sensations which can thematically relate to several scenes in the play, but which like Aeschylus' own imagery are to do with obscure and generalized emotions: fear, prophesy, defiance, desire.

But, of course, it would be ludicrous to try to establish any full equivalence between Greek tragedy and Bacon's painting. Without lessening the grandeur of the central image, Bacon brings us sharply against the distance that separates the modern world from the ancient myth, in the left-hand panel, by including a very modern and unusually distinct tubular chair, propping open the door. This immediately brings to mind T.S. Eliot, who, too, looked back to the *Oresteia*, and based on it his play *The Family Reunion*. The following lines from 'Sweeney Among the Nightingales', in a very general sense, could be cited in connection with Bacon:

> The host with someone indistinct
> Converses at the door apart
> The nightingales are singing near
> The Convent of the Sacred Heart
>
> And sang within the bloody wound
> When Agamemnon cried aloud
> And let their liquid siftings fall
> To stain the stiff dishonoured shroud.

Bacon has always considered that he was influenced by Eliot, or certainly that reading Eliot's poetry was a fruitful source, not directly of specific images that he would translate into paint, but of images which awoke a series of associations in Bacon himself and fed in that way into his painting.[43] He was particularly responsive, perhaps, to the combination in Eliot of nostalgia for classical mythology, the abruptness of modern manners, the threat of the unseen and the eruption of casual violence; Sweeney, in the poem 'Sweeney Erect',

> Tests the razor on his leg
> Waiting until the shriek subsides . . .[44]

Although not specified in the titles, other images in Bacon's painting refer to the *Oresteia*: in the central panel of the 1976 triptych (98), black birds tear the flesh of a clearly human, even living 'carcass'. Its leg is raised in just the gesture of the Agamemnon figure from the 1981 triptych, and might evoke the lines of the shocked chorus confronted by the murderous Clytemnestra:

> You empower the sisters, Fury's twins,
> Whose power tears the heart!
> Perched on the corpse your carrion raven
> Glories in her hymn . . .

The brimming bowl certainly suggests libation, and the Eumenides or Furies seem to be present. It is also possible that this image of the bird tearing flesh could be to do with the Prometheus myth. In revenge for Prometheus' act of stealing fire from the gods to give to men, he was condemned to be chained for ever to a rock with a vulture gnawing his flesh. Prometheus is the epitome of the tragic hero, both winner and loser in a hopeless battle against fate and the gods.

Bacon insists that all he wants to do is make images; people can then read into them what they will.[45] To take the first part of this apparently innocuous statement only, it is perhaps not as straightforward as it seems. From what are these images constructed? What kind of relationship with the natural world is implied? What sort of sources does he choose, and how does he treat them? What measure of factuality enters the images, and what is 'fact' measured against?

The catholicity of Bacon's sources has already been mentioned, and his acknowledged or implicit use of poetry, drama, other paintings, and photography of various kinds. Bacon himself has pointed to his use of Velasquez, Van Gogh and Ingres, which is quite explicit. Mark Roskill has instanced the borrowing of the figure of the sergeant in Manet's *Execution of the Emperor Maximilian* in his *Study of Van Gogh I*, 1956, and has suggested, surely correctly, that there may be many other such borrowings.

The issues raised by Bacon's use of photographs, with which I should like to conclude this essay, are of particular interest in his works: photographs are a different kind of visual source from the images other painters have created, and this is because of their status as record, as fact, or history. Bacon was intrigued by the 'candid camera' snaps of famous people in unguarded

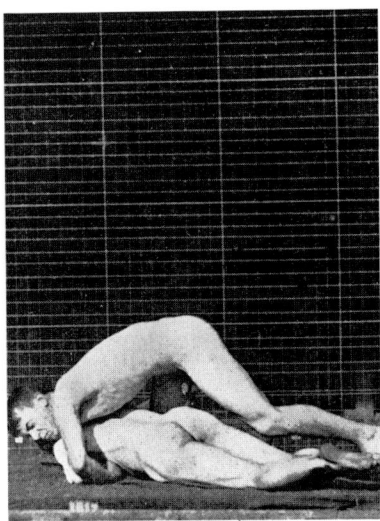

Eadweard Muybridge, photograph from
The Human Figure in Motion, 1887

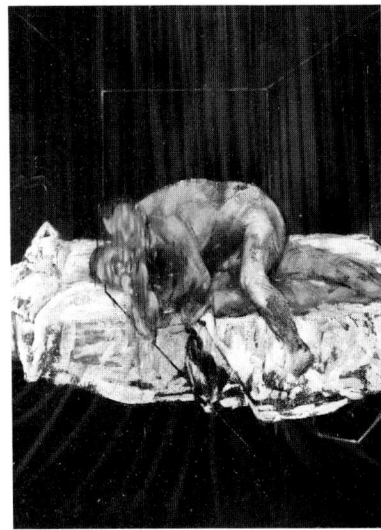

Two Figures, 1953

moments that became a source of popular amusement in the 1930s, and has also 'used' news photographs, photographs from wild-life studies, from medical books, polyphotos of himself, photographs of friends, and perhaps most significantly of all photographic studies of movement by Eadweard Muybridge. Most of this has, as John Russell said, 'been composted beyond the point of no recovery.'[46] But it is not so much the fact that he uses them, but what he does to them in using them that is interesting.

It is both because the Muybridge sources are still traceable, but also because of the special nature of these studies in relation to the real world, that Bacon's paintings based on them need special attention. Muybridge's first experiments were intended to document the actual movement of the horse, the movement of the legs while galloping. In the 1870s and 1880s, with a more sophisticated camera (he had first used a series of cameras with threads attached to their shutters which were broken and released by the horse), he turned his attention to the study of normal and abnormal locomotion using a variety of subjects. The enormous contemporary interest in his work reflects the nineteenth-century passion for and belief in scientific objectivity, and in a new kind of verisimilitude. But there was also the passion for curiosities, an element of the circus, which ran almost unconsciously beside the scientific; the wonders of nature could, after all, so easily brush the fantastic. So, among the stranger of Muybridge's studies of 'actions incidental to every day life' were 'Chicken Scared by a Torpedo', 'Man Heaving a 75 lb. Rock', and 'Man Walking, after Traumatism of the Head'. One, at least, of Muybridge's studies of abnormal movement was used by Bacon, in his study of the paralytic child walking on all fours (46).

But the first point to make is that Bacon is not so much using the photograph as attacking it, challenging its status as record or fact through his transformations. The photograph may claim to capture or present reality, but is in fact only reflective of a – restricted – visual fact. It cannot record sensations, emotions, experience or associations, above all not the intense life of the body. It is understandable that Muybridge should have so fascinated Bacon, for he was above all concerned with the body. Paintings after Muybridge include the following: *Triptych – Studies from the Human Body*, 1970 (69), *Two Figures*, 1953 (22), the dog in *Man with Dog*, 1953 (18). Bacon used Muybridge's studies of naked wrestlers several times, transforming them into a couple locked in a sexual rather than athletic embrace. The distance after all is not that great and the aggression is more emphatic in the sexual encounter. Through the studies of the wrestlers Bacon found he could reach the fact of embrace more accurately or, as he put it, return fact on to the nervous system more violently. It is not just a matter of re-fusing the movements that Muybridge so laboriously separated to reveal the greater 'reality' of movement, because the distortions of the upper body in *Two Figures* are not a matter of thickening or repeating forms to suggest physical bodily movement, as the Futurists did, but of trying to give the muscular sensation of spasm or contraction; it is sight, touch, tension, orgasm, together. It is a way of rendering visible invisible forces. Secondly, the photograph proved for Bacon an invaluable ally in the fight against cliché. Deleuze saw in Bacon a parallel with Cézanne who, unable 'to accept the ready-made clichés that came from his mental consciousness, stocked with memories and which appeared mocking at him on his canvas, spent most of his time smashing his own forms to bits.'[47] Ready-made and not subject to aesthetic convention, the photograph lies outside cliché. Bacon makes use of both the restricted and the non-aesthetic fact of the photograph, and the free marks made by accident or chance, to create the 'graph' of his painting.

Finally, the photograph, in spite of its pretensions to record, often paradoxically contains a curious slippage from reality, or from what we expect to see. Looking at photographs is often a process of discovery rather than simple recognition, and this odd slippage is often what provides Bacon with a peg or key. 'I think it's the slight remove from fact, which returns me onto the fact more violently. Through the photographic image I find myself beginning to wander into the image and unlock what I think of as its reality more than I can by looking at it. And photographs are not only points of reference, they're often triggers of ideas.'[48]

NOTES

1 Peter Fuller, 'Ludic Hope', *Vanguard*, Apr. 1984.

2 Berger's comments were made during a discussion at the ICA, a report of which by Lawrence Alloway, 'Points of View: Bacon and Balthus', was published in *Art News and Review*, 26 Jan. 1952, p. 7. The panel, chaired by David Sylvester, included Berger, Robert Melville, Michael Ayrton, Colin McInnes, Angus Wilson and Herbert Read. Berger was reported as introducing 'tangled moral considerations: we look at Bacon instead of going to Belsen, and this is not a "constructive attitude". He complained of a lack of indignation in Bacon's art which does not stir the conscience.'

3 David Sylvester, *Interviews with Francis Bacon 1962–1979*, London and New York, 1980, p. 81.

4 Sylvester, p. 56.

5 Sylvester, p. 65.

6 Sylvester, p. 60.

7 Andrew Forge, 'The Paint of Screams', *Art News*, New York, Oct. 1963, pp. 38–41, 55–6.

8 *Francis Bacon: Recent Paintings*, Marlborough-Gerson Gallery, New York, 1968.

9 Sylvester, p. 22.

10 Gilles Deleuze, *Francis Bacon: Logique de la sensation*, Paris, 1981.

11 Sylvester, p. 58. (The authenticity of this Rembrandt is in doubt.)

12 Sylvester, p. 56.

13 See Giacometti's letter to Pierre Matisse, 1947, transl. in *Alberto Giacometti*, New York, 1965.

14 Mark Roskill, 'Francis Bacon as a Mannerist', *Art International*, New York, 25 Sept. 1963, pp. 44–8.

15 Sylvester, p. 82.

16 'Francis Bacon: The Authority of Flesh', *Art Forum*, New York, Summer 1975.

17 Sylvester, p. 133–4.

18 F. Nietzsche, *The Birth of Tragedy and The Genealogy of Morals*, transl. Francis Golffing, New York, 1956, p. 10.

19 Ibid. Nietzsche argued that pessimism was not of necessity a sign of decadence: 'Is there such a thing as a *strong* pessimism? A penchant of the mind for what is hard, terrible, evil, dubious in existence, arising from a plethora of health, a plenitude of being? Could it be, perhaps, that the very feeling of superabundance created its own kind of suffering: a temerity of penetration, hankering for the enemy (the worthwhile enemy) so as to prove its strength, to experience at last what it means to fear something? What meaning did the tragic myths have for the Greeks during the period of their greatest power and courage?'

20 Deleuze, *Francis Bacon: Logique de la sensation*, Paris, 1981, p. 31.

21 'Dureté optimiste'. J.-P. Sartre, *L'Existentialisme est un humanisme*, Paris, 1946 (English transl. *Existentialism and Humanism*, London, 1948).

22 Sylvester, p. 11.

23 Sylvester, p. 91.

24 Sylvester, p. 11.

25 See, for example, Michel Leiris, *Francis Bacon: Full Face and in Profile*, New York and Oxford, 1983.

26 André Breton, 'Second manifeste du surréalisme', *La Révolution surréaliste*, Paris, no. 12, 15 Dec. 1929, p. 16.

27 See, for example, Sylvester, Roskill, 'Francis Bacon as a Mannerist', *Art International*, New York, 25 Sept. 1963, pp. 44–8, John Russell, *Francis Bacon*, London and New York, 1979, Robert Melville, 'Francis Bacon', *Horizon*, London, Dec. 1949/Jan. 1950. Melville also instances Buñuel and Dalí's silent Surrealist film, *Un Chien andalou* (a film which deeply impressed both Bacon and Bataille).

28 Sylvester, p. 35.

29 Georges Bataille, 'La Bouche', *Documents*, Paris, no. 5, 1930, pp. 299–300.

30 Julia Kristeva, 'Bataille, l'expérience et la pratique', *Bataille* (Direction Philippe Sollers: Communications Roland Barthes, et al.), Paris, 1973.

31 Aeschylus, 'The Eumenides', *The Oresteia*, transl. R. Fagles, London, 1976, l. 50.

32 This series began in 1948 and was numbered successively into 1949; normally numbering is successive within a year.

33 Sylvester, p. 50.

34 Sylvester, p. 48.

35 Sigmund Freud, *The Interpretation of Dreams*, transl. J. Strachey, London, 1954, p. 387.

36 Bacon has talked of his interest K.C. Clark's *Positioning in Radiography*, London, 1939.

37 Sylvester, p. 107.

38 Aeschylus, 'The Eumenides', l. 252. In Fagles' translation (see note 31, above) this line is rendered as 'the reek of human blood – it's laughter to my heart!', which is a rationalization of Aeschylus' shocking image. The line as Bacon quotes it is translated in W. Stanford, *Aeschylus in His Style*, Dublin, 1942.

39 Georges Bataille, 'Abattoir', *Documents*, Paris, no. 6, Nov. 1929, p. 329.

40 Sylvester, p. 23.

41 Sylvester, p. 48.

42 F. Nietzsche, 'A Critical Backward Glance', preface of 1886 to *The Birth of Tragedy*, in *The Birth of Tragedy and The Genealogy of Morals*, transl. Francis Golffing, New York, 1956.

43 A detailed study of Bacon's imagery in relation to T.S. Eliot has recently been published by Rolf Læssøe, which pays particular attention to the *Triptych Inspired by T.S. Eliot's Poem 'Sweeney Agonistes'* (1967), and to parallels between Bacon's themes and Eliot's play *The Family Reunion*. Læssøe, 'Francis Bacon and T.S. Eliot', *Hafnia*, Papers in the History of Art, Copenhagen, no. 9, 1983.

44 T.S. Eliot, *The Complete Poems and Plays*, London, 1969.

45 Conversation with the author, Sept. 1984.

46 John Russell, *Francis Bacon*, London and New York, 1979, p. 65. Russell gives an excellent account of Muybridge and of Bacon's use of his photographs.

47 D.H. Lawrence, 'Introduction to These Paintings' (1929), *Selected Essays*, London, 1950, p. 337.

48 Sylvester, p. 30.

Andrew Forge

ABOUT BACON

Among Francis Bacon's recent paintings is one based on Ingres' *Oedipus and the Sphinx*. Like most of them, it has a degree of calm that is unfamiliar in his work. The flesh of both the Sphinx and her interlocutor is pale and tightly pulled. Oedipus, bottom right, appears as a thick-necked bruiser in singlet and shorts. He has kicked one leg up on to a pedestal like an upturned book-case, as if to adjust the blood-stained bandage that wraps his foot and calf. The other leg, supporting him, thrusts out of the corner of the canvas, the thigh powerfully flexed. The foot at the end of the bloody leg is reversed : it is his right leg but his left foot, the big toe downstage from us.

His limbs are massive, but even more massive is his short neck, a stubby cylinder nearly twice as thick as his calf. The head sprouts out of it, a flattened half-transparent knob, the sheen on jaw and cheek floating over the rounded poll as though glassy axe blows had uncovered the movement of the face against the light. The tender pink orifice of the ear is low down, at the hinge of the jaw.

Sphinx and man are at opposite sides of a room. The walls are of flat cyclamen pink, the floor beige. The Sphinx is half out of the left side of the frame. Its torso is like a light urn on slender footing, its breasts and the root of its wings smoothly turned. This suggestion of symmetry seems to speak of an alternative anatomy, opposite to the man's virile maimed weight. The Sphinx's neck is thick like the man's but smoothly graded like the lid of an urn in contrast to Oedipus' brown heavily modelled stump. The Sphinx is an apparition outside time. Its head is turned towards Oedipus alertly, as if to focus its glance upon him, but its face is veiled. It is as though the face – the face of a handsome, full-lipped man – was encapsulated within the head, screened by an opalescent covering. The stare we look for is withheld.

In Ingres' painting there is a witness to the encounter with the Sphinx, a companion of Oedipus' who turns with a fearful gesture before running off down the hillside. Bacon's witness is more central. Between the two pink walls there is a door open to the darkness of the night. Set into the door is a plate glass sheet covering three quarters of the opening. Hung at the top of the glass, smashed against it, crawling up it or looking at us through it, is one of those stump-pawed, pod-bodied chimeras that Bacon has identified as Eumenides. The body ends in a long crest or tail and a round hole – eye or anus – cleanly drilled as if by Black and Decker or bullet.

This being, too, is bloody. One could picture it as a fragment of offal thrown and stuck, half dried, to the glass. But it is avidly alive too. A white arrow points to the centre of its bloodiness, and beyond to the marble-like breast of the Sphinx. An ellipse, like an enormous slide-frame, partially encloses the creature. Similar devices frame Oedipus, enclosing his torso and hanging over his broken foot like a halo.

In Ingres, Oedipus and Sphinx stare intently into each other's eyes, their hands almost touching. Oedipus has put his question and, his eye focused to a point, is listening intently to her reply. The Sphinx is speaking, her head arched like an angry swan, her wings erect. Her face has that look of flashing fury that opera singers take on at moments of greatest projection. In Bacon, it is doubtful whether the question has or will ever be put into words. It is implicit, not in Oedipus' gesture – his bandage absorbs his attention – but in the Sphinx's turned head, and in the memory of the earlier picture which haunts our reading.

In his conversations with David Sylvester (surely the richest discussions between artist and critic ever recorded) Bacon tends to frame his statements dialectically, opposing will and intuition, chance and judgment, the organic and the artificial and so on. Reading him, we are brought back again and again to the thought that the friction between opposites is essential to him and that unless an issue can be felt to be grinding between these either/ors it has no vitality

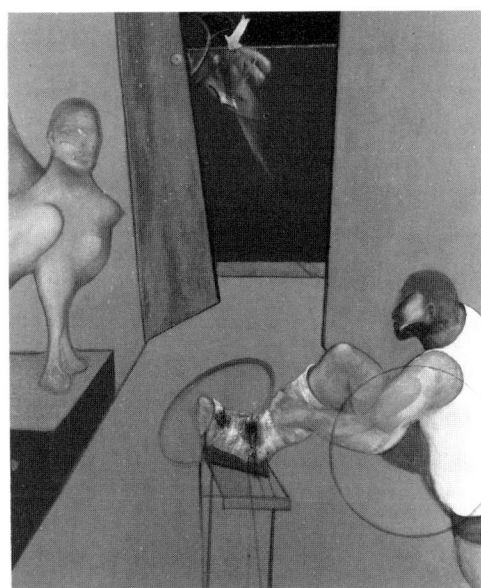

Ingres, *Oedipus and the Sphinx*, 1808. Oil on canvas. The Louvre, Paris

Bacon, *Oedipus and the Sphinx after Ingres*, 1983

for him. Everything must be loved or loathed. The last thing he is looking for is remission from this tension. 'Friction' is too weak – it is the incompatibility of opposites that counts. Resolution goes with comfort.

His painting draws us willy nilly into these polarities. It just is not possible to enter his paintings in a spirit of aesthetic neutrality, to see them in their fullness beside other painting. (At a superficial level this is more easily done simply by invoking 'Bacon's world'; that is to say, by reducing all his paintings to more or less successful illustrations of nightmare.)

At the very centre of his pictures is his engagement with paint and its power to give back an image. Chance and its exalted manipulation are here at work in white heat. In opposition to this, framing but not mediating, his critical faculty constructs an environment. The pulsating jet of the figure is shown against a flat and brittle background, often cursorily and even mechanically painted, within which various pieces of furniture and graphic devices work as signs, seeming almost to mock the possibility of deeper connections within the fabric of the painting. Figure and field oppose each other as intuition opposes calculation.

A weak parallel would be with some eighteenth-century formal portrait (a Reynolds, for example) in which the vivid particulars of the head are set into a conventional framework of columns, curtains and distant landscape, and we feel called upon to read the picture at two distinct levels, the formulaic and the particular. In such an example, of course, the two poles of the painting are carried along by an acknowledged convention. We know that that society knew what it meant by a portrait.

But what does Bacon 'mean' by his disjunctures, by the unyielding contrast between his figures and their surroundings? His own answer – the only answer an artist could honourably give – would be 'nothing'. It would be more to the point to put the question to ourselves, to the imaginary Bacon that we construct when we look at his pictures. What does he mean?

One answer can be tried by passing the matter over to life. What states of attention or perception does his painting speak to? Watching a boxing match, our eyes are on the fighters. The ring has importance only as a limit to their manoeuvres. We are aware of its ropes, corners and open centre only as they stand for possibilities of advance and retreat, movement or in-fighting. One does not *contemplate* a rope or a spray of sweat on the canvas while watching a fight. How much less does the fighter? The livelier the action, it seems fair to generalize, the closer the patterns of our attention come to his.

If this is a useful figure for the way things work when we look at a Bacon, it tokens a connection between experience and painting, between the dynamics of perception and the construction of a picture that is of a kind unlike anything else in painting.

It opposes itself to all those qualities of unity, simultaneity and internal responsiveness that would seem to be indispensable within the tradition of the art. Disjunctions in a figure painting by Picasso or de Kooning, for instance, whether distortions from normative semblance or breaks in the convention like a collaged mouth or an abrupt transition from flat to modelled paint, have the effect of moving us to see the whole canvas as a figure. They enhance and extend pictorial unity rather than withhold it. They do not repel aesthetic contemplation but stimulate and invite it, however challengingly.

But with Bacon the movement is always inwards, towards the strenuous centre.

When David Sylvester asked him about the contradiction between the painterly figures and their flat bright backgrounds, Bacon told him: 'Well, that may be because I hate a homely atmosphere, and I always feel that *malerisch* painting has too homely a background. I want to isolate the image and take it away from the interior and the home.'

I cannot have been the only reader of this passage to have sat up at the word homely. In Freud's paper on *The Uncanny* (1919) he approaches his subject from two directions. One is the etymology of the words *unheimlich* ('uncanny' in Strachey's translation) and *heimlich*, 'homely'. The other is the hypothesis that the uncanny is experienced when something is uncovered, throwing the mind back to earlier mental states, long since laid to rest. The idea of a double, for example, fills us with a sense of the uncanny because it throws us back to earlier states of primary narcissism when we imagined a double for ourselves as a defence against destruction or death. Or, the uncanny experience of coincidence when numbers and names repeat themselves in a way that we cannot rationalize and we are involuntarily thrown back into re-experiencing an infantile belief in magical omnipotence.

As to the word homely, Freud tells us that the German *heimlich*, whose first meaning is the obvious one (comforting, soothing, intimate, domestic), has a second, less cosy meaning. It means secret, concealed, hidden, and by extension, sinister. One of his exemplary quotations from German literature reads: 'You call it unheimlich, we call it heimlich.' Is it absurd to read a similar ambivalence into Bacon's 'homely'? That is, to understand his hatred to be levelled both at cosiness and complacency and also at concealment and secrecy. There is a harsh puritan undertone here, reviling comfort and hypocrisy in a single word, as though, to him, the fitting-togetherness of painterly unity falsely predicates an integrated world.

'The intimacy of the image against a very stark background.' The intimacy he is talking about is invoked every time one makes the effort to read his images closely. It is the intimacy of nakedness and exposure, not the intimacy of comfort. Years ago I wrote that for me the intimacy of Bacon's paintings owed little to 'the overall view of things, but rather to its opposite – a particular experience of hunting semblance with paint. His hunt is lived out in time on the canvas and it is this which one lives out in one's own present time in front of the canvas too. With him, each addition or scrubbed cancellation alters the face that is looking back at him, bringing it closer, or not, to his bated attention – and so it is too on our side. The distortions of his heads, which at first sight look like ghastly wounds, have to be gathered up, pieced together, until the head looks right, intact. The price is the stability of one's viewpoint. . . A kind of closeness has to be risked: not a physical closeness to the picture concerned but a psychic closeness to the "head".'

At the beginning of the essay on *The Uncanny*, Freud says that 'the better orientated in his environment a person is, the less readily will he get the impression of something uncanny in regard to the objects and events in it.'

Pictures image a place for us in the world. The disturbing violence of Bacon's work is not limited to its local imagery. It is present in the contrast between 'intimate' image and 'stark' background, and the violent challenge to stability thrown off by it. Whatever it is that his pictures amount to is to be found only at the risk of disorientation. There are certain pictures in the Van Gogh series of the late 1950s in which he attempted a version of painterly all-overness (32, 33). For all their furiousness, there is not much in them of tension.

At a certain point many of Bacon's paintings began to be of named individuals, the painter's friends. Faces became particular where previously they had been anonymous. Anyone who knows his paintings knows his cast of models. They turn up again and again and are instantly recognizable. Talking about the importance Bacon ascribed to different categories of subject matter, David Sylvester asked him whether he was interested in restoring the traditional hierarchies which placed figure composition at the highest level, then portraiture, then landscape and so on, down. Bacon said that he was, except that 'at the moment, as things are so difficult, portraits come first.' It is a haunting, magnificent answer.

What are the things that are so difficult? The most obvious is surely that for a modern painter there is no access to type, at least not in a straight un-ironic way. Only advertisements use type with any conviction and I suppose that even here it is the *use* of types that we attend to, rather than the types themselves. Yet a traditional portrait relies upon type, is founded upon it. The sitter is seen first 'as' an admiral, a faithful wife, a scholar, a statesman, and the role provides the formal and communicative frame within which the individual features come to life. Occasionally – one thinks of Holbein drawings or Hals or Goya – features and frame become so mysteriously intertwined that there is no parting them. Reading the painting becomes a lesson in human history.

We may be sure that Bacon's sense of what constitutes a likeness does not include the social mask. Everything that he has ever said or done rejects it. If formality plays a part in his view of others, as it obviously does, this has to be distinguished from convention and jolly social agreement.

By the same token he rejects the conventions that have dominated the art of his lifetime. I am not thinking merely of his dismissal of abstract painting as fashionable pattern making, but rather that in his claim for an art of the human figure he has made his stand on likeness. This is his scandal.

If he had ever had a formal training as a painter, we can be quite sure that sooner or later someone would have told him to 'forget the features. Concentrate on the form.' Serious painters of the generation that would have taught him would look to what they would have called the essentials, for it was there that true likeness resided. The gap between Sargent and Cézanne, between Sir William Orpen and Matisse was unbridgeable. Dimples, moist eyes, half smiles were taboo.

Bacon affronts this taboo. Sometimes his people seem to be all appearance, nothing else. Sometimes they seem to be made of nothing but their own expression: faces dominate heads, features dominate faces. Sometimes the features themselves seem to be nothing but shine, sheen, surface, there in a flickering instant, not to be grasped. Sometimes they are holes.

If that imaginary teacher of painting – I picture an earnest post-Impressionist, possibly familiar with Matisse's *Notes of a Painter* – if he is allowed to continue with his lesson he will go on to liken the human head to a block; and to suggest that when that block is achieved in its full solidity, and only then, the individual features can be drawn in. He will urge the building of that block to be undertaken with logic. Each colour change will construct a plane and the whole will hang together. If this, then that.

Bacon takes us in an opposite direction. The head in the *Portrait of Isabel Rawsthorne Standing in a Street in Soho*, solid though it is, is certainly not built around anything sequentially: it comes at us all at once like a grimace. We are drawn into a closer and closer reading of it and what is given us is less a logical building up of form than its opposite, a demolition. Her eyes, whose glaring address is an intense focal point in the painting, seem hardly to have been painted at all. The pupils are like openings onto a dark substratum, holes left in a thin veil of white that smears over the darkness. We are far more aware of what has been taken away than of what has been added. The lower face, jaw and mouth, comes across out of residual wipes of paint dragged like cobwebs over a blood-red base. Cheek bone and brow, neck and nose come across out of swipes in which fleshy pink is shadowed with a gloomy Prussian blue, swipes that do not so much make forms as manipulate some expectation of them. Crucial edges – the defining line of cheek bone, jaw and neck – are made negatively with strokes of black that invade from the outside, cutting into a head that is all look, all presence and whose anatomy seems to consist precisely of those moves in paint become flesh.

These moves work continually against the grain. The mouth with its full, determined lips, has a massive scale to it; yet there is no jaw to support it. It must find its place as best it can

Portrait of George Dyer Riding a Bicycle, 1966

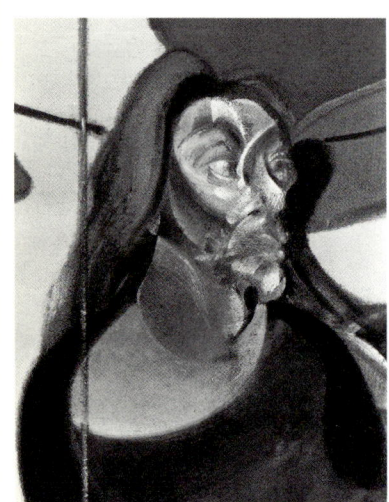

Portrait of Isabel Rawsthorne Standing in a Street in Soho (detail), 1967

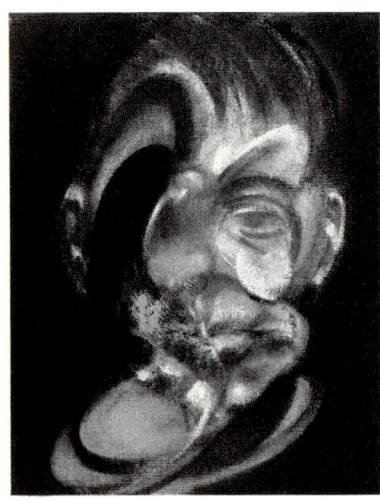

Self Portrait, 1973

between the highlit tip of the chin and the nose, whose transparent lobe spreads half across her cheek. The forehead, with its frame of dark hair, is split, as if by some massive displacement of the eyebrow which now curves diagonally down between the nose and the near eye. This dark form, which reappears again and again in Bacon's portraits, allows for a multiplicity of readings. Often, as here, it is solid. Its outer edge is lit. It makes me think of the words 'raising a welt'. Sometimes in other paintings it looks like a bone wrenched out from somewhere else, a chop bone suddenly necessary in the making of a head. In more than one portrait this dark, splitting line takes a form like a curved spoon, reminding one of some sort of surgical instrument.

Whatever one might choose to call it – and to name it at all is merely to play at taming Bacon's wordless imagery – it is clear that repeatedly the moment arrives when he needs to divide the head he is painting, to split it up, to detach it from solid, free-standing expectations, to render it as though only his attention to it guaranteed its existence.

If we allow this curving edge, this misplaced eyebrow, to control the way we read the Rawsthorne head, we notice that it throws our attention towards the side of the head furthest from us. It is as though a new head is being indicated, narrower, more reserved, less angry in its glance. If we switch our attention to the whole head, returning the far side to its place in the whole, we are likely to experience a jolt, as if the change in our reading corresponded to some sudden change of mood in the painting.

It is an effect that reappears many times in Bacon: the most explicit instance being in the *Portrait of George Dyer Riding a Bicycle*, 1966, in which his full face is framed by his own profile painted flatly and on a larger scale, and his head switches through ninety degrees according to the focus of our attention. The re-reading possible in the smaller heads tends to be more complex and more surprising. There is a self portrait of 1973 where a black blob something like an exclamation mark streams down from the painter's right eye, obscuring it. The aspect of the head is full face: both sides are visible, both ears are in place. The blob flows with the direction of the nose and there is a strong invitation to see it as creating a contour for the nose which is now felt to be in profile. The head turns and returns. The expression changes. Somehow the sense of stoic steadiness becomes more and more ingrained in these features that at first sight seemed pulpy and formless.

A lock of hair, a shadow; or merely some arbitrary jet of paint will set up a kind of internal contour, inviting revisions. It will twist the central axis of the head, key to its symmetry, wrenching the armature out of true. The scale of individual features changes under our reading, coming and going, breaking down the distance between us and the head, rendering it malleable in contradiction to the constant, repetitive size of the heads which invariably nearly fill a canvas of 16 by 12 inches.

Features find themselves within an endlessly varied range of paint. An eye, a nostril will be defined with the precision of a driven nail. Elsewhere they will be merely adumbrated, hardly to be made out of a general cloud of flesh, a pinkness that hovers over the grey-brown linen of the support like a formless culture spreading across a gauze. Greyish pink paint seems somehow to have arrived in its place by its own agency, to have grown into the painting. Sometimes it feels as if it had been delicately blotted into the canvas like powder. Sometimes it falls into regular striations, the imprint of a corduroy rag.

These ribbed passages alone offer a wide variety of readings. They introduce a formal register against which the threat of formlessness is steadied. They bring the skin sometimes to the very surface of the canvas. At others they set up a cage or screen behind which lips or the sliding plane of a cheek can be made out.

A similar part is played, though a more aggressive one, by the mysterious circles and ellipses that often hover in front of the heads or are embedded in them as if by plastic surgery. Although they often carve out directions, slicing the air around a head or nailing it more firmly into position, they always carry with them the double implication of a lens – an intensifier of sight – and a hole drilled. Their prototype is the shattered pince-nez of the nursemaid in Eisenstein's film *Battleship Potemkin* (see p. 15). They have gathered other affinities, with mouths, nostrils, cameras, watchglasses, muzzles and the sectioned tubes of the viscera.

Eyes are crucial. Sometimes the sockets alone will work to set up the essential configuration of the face, leaving the direction of the glance open, implicit in a dark stare. Sometimes the eyes are given as the plainest almonds that could almost be interchangeable, right to left, and whose gaze is less particular to the model than it is to us and our own stare back. At the other extreme, eyes are particularized with startling vividness, functioning as keys to our reading of the rest of the head or the whole figure. In the painting of *George Dyer Crouching*, 1966, the figure, scrunched up at the end of a diving board, is formless at first sight. Then one hits upon an eye, flat on the side of the head, precisely defined, unwinking, dryly glittering. At once the figure and head emerge from formlessness and fall into detailed organization. The weight and thickness of the thighs, the downward stretch of the arm, the massive crest of muscle across the shoulders, the motionless concentration of the lowered head, all seem to leap out of the paint, triggered by the hard saurian eye which, as with some fantastic knobbly lizards, seems to be embedded like a living jewel in material that follows another order of form.

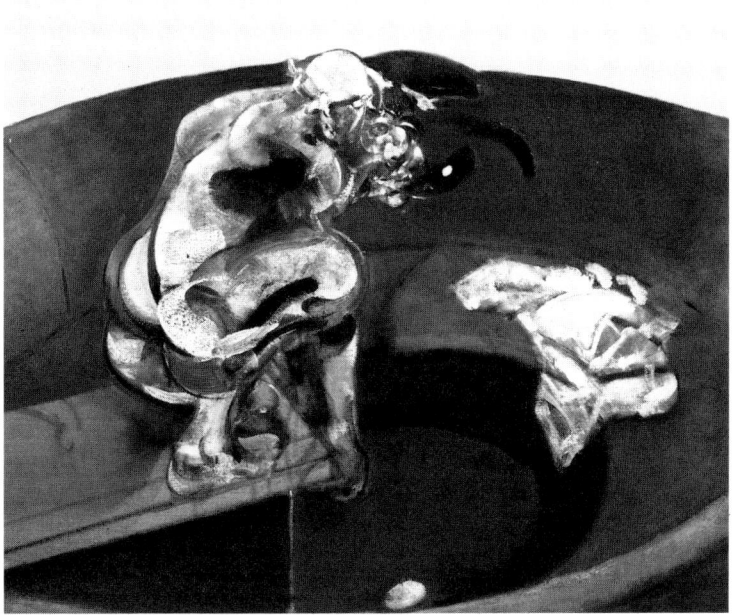

George Dyer Crouching (detail), 1966

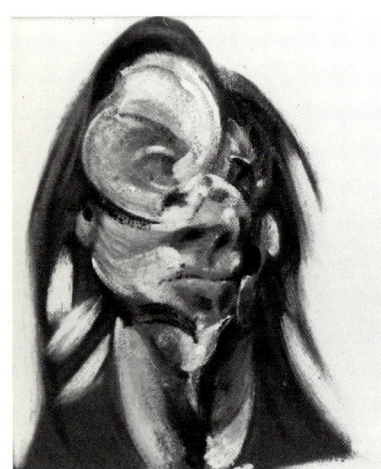

Study of Isabel Rawsthorne, 1965

Study of Henrietta Moraes, 1969

Self Portrait, 1971

In many of the portraits of Isabel Rawsthorne her eyes glide off sideways with an alert, measuring look. In portraits of Henrietta Moraes the eyes are usually cast down. Rawsthorne's image provokes expectations of words, of wit and instant exchange. Moraes' calls up more ancient relationships and slower-moving physical power that draws in to itself.

The eyes are downcast in many of the self portraits, too. The sense of involuntary empathy that is inescapable in reading Bacon's heads is amplified in these cases and turned back on itself. The movements implied by the manipulation of the features begin to feel like the movements of states of mind, born physically. There is a self portrait of 1971 in which the eyes are lowered but just open. They have a certain sensual weight, the look of someone giving himself up to pain or exhaustion. It is the only image I know in which distortions begin to 'feel' like violence actually suffered. Far less extreme in its distortions than many other heads, the paint comes over like a beating.

'My ideal', Bacon told David Sylvester on the subject of his portraits, 'would really be just to pick up a handful of paint and throw it at the canvas and hope that the portrait was there.' He must have meant to say '. . . and *find* that the portrait was there.' The word hope slipped out, referring back to 'my ideal' – what I hoped for. But its presence in that declaration points in another direction too.

Suppose this ideal had been realized and the thrown paint had given him the likeness that he longed for. What really would have happened? Would the paint have made this particular face on its own? Magic is being hoped for, and that hope is perhaps just the purest form of a hope for a state of mind in which unstructured paint can be seen as being depictive. 'Seeing as' implies a drive, a particular quality of hope, a willed hallucination, pushing its way out towards the inchoate paint, finding likeness in it. Such a likeness would be recognized all at once, not built up out of a deliberated structure but suddenly given back.

This seems to match something of our own experience in looking at these portraits, not that we see the paint, for all its accidentals, as random. In the great portrait of Michel Leiris, the narrow one, his mouth faces us but then slides away to the left. His head is square on to us, but then turns and slices back obliquely. It feels as if we are both in and out of the painting – being in it and looking at it at the same time. Twisting, sliding, slicing are internal sensations. We hit upon Leiris' face over against a physiognomy that is inside us. Bacon's manipulations work upon an inner knowledge that is laid down among the very foundations of how we see. The raw chops, the open soft palate, the stumps of teeth and glistening gums that are horrible in certain heads seen from the outside, become nothing less than our entry to likeness as we explore. And paint is the essential intermediary. What we experience as we move from the right side of Leiris' jaw to the left is a continuous unbroken identity of paint and flesh. Flesh shifts, but whether it does so 'under our eyes' – or somewhere else – is hard to say.

The small portraits dispense with *mise en scène*. Nothing cushions us from the painful interiorized discovery of likeness that I have tried to describe. Academic distinctions between head and expression have as little meaning here as do qualities of overall painterliness. Heads and their features flow in and out of each other restlessly. However, this 'movement' has nothing to do with the accounts of movement given by a Balla or a Duchamp. There is nothing cinematic in Bacon, at least not in the obvious sense of a discrete form being in motion in front of a fixed viewpoint. If the influence of the camera has to be addressed, it must be in less literal terms.

Snapshots never let us forget the enigma of likeness. Each frozen image wrenched out of time – blind, split, mouth stuffed with potato salad – reminds us that we see and recognize each other in time. These stolen images bring home to us that what we mean by a person's appearance – the constant that remains in spite of aging or split-second grimacing, nearness or distance – is something that we hold to within a continuum. Furthermore, we are reminded that our idea of what somebody 'really' looks like holds steady for just as long as we take it for granted. Once we address ourselves to it directly, everything begins to wobble. Because the background against which we form an idea of the person is nothing less than our view of the world – a world that includes ourselves. This psychical background is symbolized in painting by the perceptual background. Once convention is broken and the plasticity of the

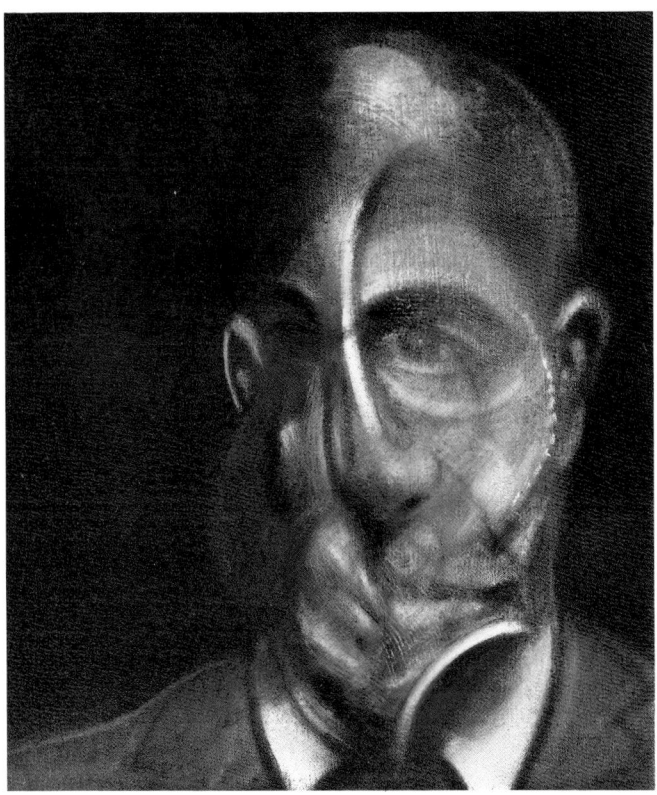

Portrait of Michel Leiris, 1976

background is admitted, the very appearance of other people becomes as mysterious as reality itself. This century is not short of instances where that background has collapsed so catastrophically that human likeness, identity even, has lost its firm outlines.

The camera, continually breaching the flow of time, breaks up the unexamined continuity of the background and, in so doing, gives it back to us in the form of a question.

The triptych arrangement that Bacon uses so often both in his major compositions and in his portrait studies contributes to the formal frame with which he isolates the main events of his painting. It has a particular stability: a centre supported by wings. With the portraits, it holds a promise of inclusiveness. Bacon has compared them to police records – left side, full-face, right side – although he does not always use this structure. But there is another invitation in the triple form, to read it sequentially, as though to 'pick up' an event or to follow out a gesture; to see it, in other words, rather like a film strip. This expectation leads us nowhere.

Nothing happens in his triptychs except what is revealed to us in our interior reading of the paint. The heads, for all their recognizability, one canvas to the next, remain isolated from each other. Similarities between one image and the next, the normal points of departure for a kinetic reading, lead us deeper and deeper into the particular realization of the head and further from an event, an imagined span of time that would unify them or explain their diverse expressions. What Bacon has learned from Muybridge – from his sequences as distinct from the individual frames that have contributed so crucially to his imagery – is the opposite of what one might expect: less a matter of time captured than of time ruptured.

The disjunction of action in his large paintings is notorious. Isolated pictorially, his figures never signal to each other across the brittle wastes of their environment. They are as alone as dying men in a row of hospital cots.

Again we sense an austere refusal on Bacon's part, and a rejection of comfort. Just as the painting refuses internal continuities, so does the event pictured refuse the connecting links of narrative. If one pair of eyes met another, if one pose slid into its next stage, if one gesture had a consequence, if Oedipus had only lifted his head to address the Sphinx, then something could have been felt to have happened that we could watch from the outside. But the homely boundaries of a story are refused. The dream remains untold, its tensions undischarged, to be dreamed another time and another time and another time.

CHRONOLOGY

1909
Born in Dublin, 28 October, of English parents, the second of five children.
Suffers from asthma as a child and has no conventional schooling.

1925
Leaves home to go to London.

1927–8
Travels to Berlin, stays for two months only, then on to Paris where he occasionally secures commissions for interior decoration. Visits a Picasso exhibition at the Paul Rosenberg Gallery which greatly impresses him and inspires him to start making drawings and watercolours.

1929
Returns to London. Exhibits in his Queensbury Mews studio furniture and rugs made from his own designs. Begins painting in oils.

1930
Arranges a joint exhibition in his studio with Roy de Maistre, showing furniture as well as paintings and gouaches.

1931
Gradually abandons his work as a decorator in order to devote himself to painting.

1933
Paints *Crucifixion 1933* which is reproduced in Herbert Read's *Art Now*.

1934
Stages his first one-man show at the Transition Gallery, Sunderland House, London.

1936
Submits some work to the International Surrealist Exhibition. It is rejected as 'not sufficiently surreal'.

1937
Takes part in an important group exhibition 'Young British Painters', at Agnews, London, organized by his friend Eric Hall.

1941–4
Destroys nearly all his earlier works. Declared unfit for military service and is assigned to Civil Defence (ARP).

1944–5
Resumes painting and executes the triptych *Three Studies for Figures at the Base of a Crucifixion*. The triptych is acquired by the Tate Gallery in 1953.

1945–6
Exhibits *Figure in a Landscape* and *Figure Study II* in group exhibitions held at the Lefevre and Redfern Galleries.

1946–50
Lives mainly in Monte Carlo. Friendship with Graham Sutherland.

1948
Alfred H. Barr purchases *Painting 1946* for the Museum of Modern Art, New York. Begins painting the series of *Heads*.

1949
One-man show at the Hanover Gallery, London, who become his agent for the next ten years.

1950
Teaches briefly at the Royal College of Art as deputy for John Minton. Travels to South Africa to visit his mother.

1951–5
Changes studios several times. For a short time (1953) shares a house with David Sylvester.

1952
Exhibits landscapes inspired by Africa and the South of France.

1953
First one-man show outside Britain at Durlacher Brothers, New York. Paints *Two Figures* (The Wrestlers).

1954
Paints the *Man in Blue* series.

1955
First retrospective exhibition at the Institute of Contemporary Arts, London. Paints portraits of the collectors Robert and Lisa Sainsbury, who become his patrons.

1956
Visits Tangier to see his friend Peter Lacey.

1957
First exhibition in Paris at the Galerie Rive Droite. Exhibits the Van Gogh series at the Hanover Gallery, London.

1958
First one-man exhibitions in Italy. Signs contract with Marlborough Fine Art, London.

1959
Exhibition at the V São Paulo Bienal.

1960
First exhibition at Marlborough Fine Art, London.

1962
Paints his first large triptych, *Three Studies for a Crucifixion*, acquired by the Solomon R. Guggenheim Museum, New York. Major retrospective exhibition at the Tate Gallery and in Mannheim, Turin and Zürich.

1963–4
Retrospective exhibition at the Solomon R. Guggenheim Museum, New York, and the Art Institute of Chicago.

1964
Friendship with George Dyer. Executes triptych *Three Figures in a Room*.

1965
Paints *Crucifixion* triptych.

1966
Exhibits at Galerie Maeght, Paris, and Marlborough Fine Art, London.

1967
Awarded the Painting Prize at the 1967 Pittsburgh International and the Rubens Prize by the City of Siegen.

1971–2
Important retrospective exhibition at the Grand Palais, Paris, and the Kunsthalle, Düsseldorf. Death in Paris of George Dyer (1971). Paints *Triptych 1971*.

1972–4
Executes series of three large triptychs influenced by the death of George Dyer.

1975
Major exhibition selected by Henry Geldzahler at the Metropolitan Museum of Art, New York.

1977
Exhibition at Claude Bernard, Paris. Another at the Museum of Modern Art, Mexico.

1978
Exhibition at the March Foundation, Madrid, and Joan Miró Foundation, Barcelona.

1980
Exhibits at the Marlborough Gallery, New York.

1983
Touring retrospective exhibition in Japan, organized by the Museum of Modern Art, Tokyo.

1984
Exhibits at Galerie Maeght, Paris, and Marlborough Gallery, New York.

1985
Lives and works in London.

PLATES

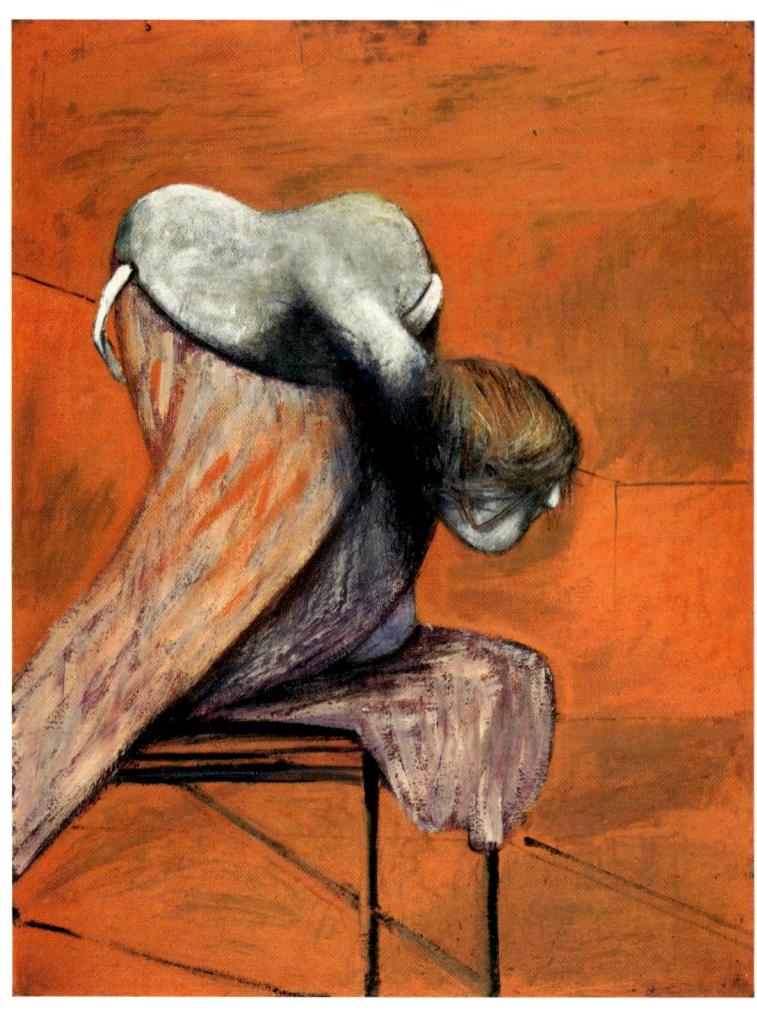

Three Studies for Figures at the Base of a Crucifixion 1944 (1)

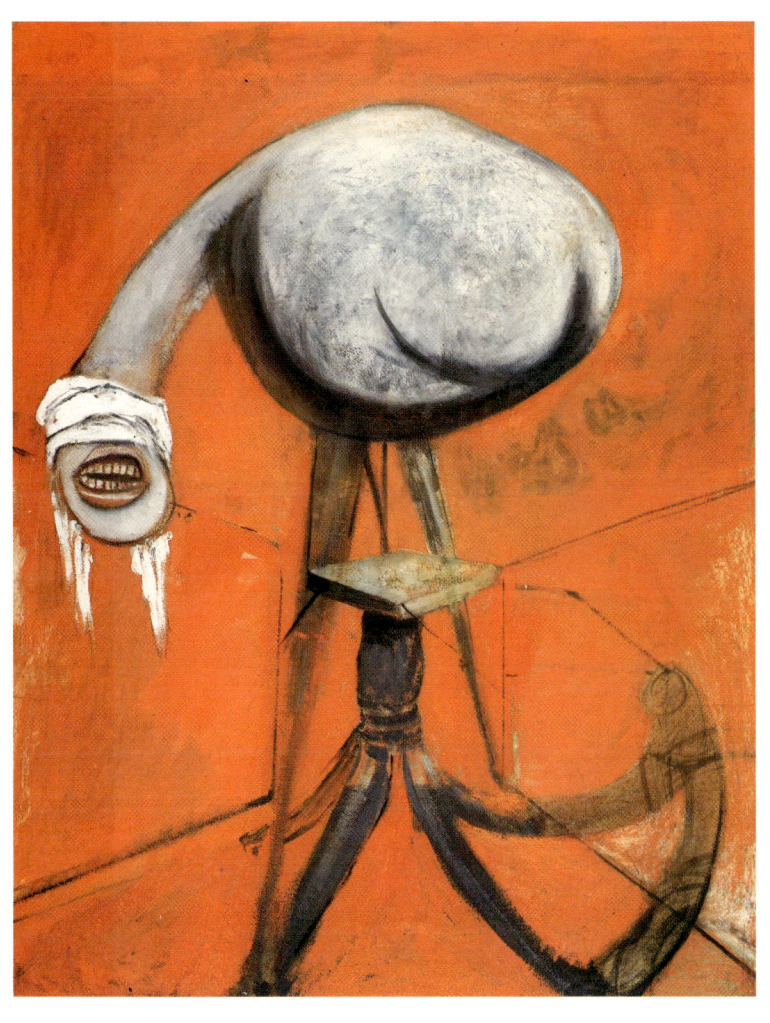

Figure in a Landscape 1945 (2)

Painting 1946 (5)

Figure Study I 1945–6 (3)

Figure Study II 1945–6 (4)

Head I 1948 (6)

Head II 1949 (7)

Head III 1949 (8)

Study for Portrait 1949 (Man in a Blue Box) (11)

Head VI 1949 (9)

Pope I 1951 (12)

Pope II 1951 (13)

Study from the Human Body 1949 (10)

Study for Crouching Nude 1952 (14)

Study of a Figure in a Landscape 1952 (15)

Man with Dog 1953 (18)

Sphinx I 1953 (19)

Study after Velasquez's Portrait of Pope Innocent X 1953 (16)

Two Figures 1953 (22)

Study of a Baboon 1953 (20)

Study for a Portrait 1953 (17)

Three Studies of the Human Head 1953 (21)

Study for a Portrait 1953 (23)

Two Figures in the Grass 1954 (24)

Chimpanzee 1955 (29)

Study for Portrait II
(after the Life Mask of William Blake) 1955 (27)

Study for Portrait III
(after the Life Mask of William Blake) 1955 (28)

Figure with Meat 1954 (25)

Pope 1954 (26)

Study for Figure IV 1956–7 (31)

Study for Portrait of Van Gogh II 1957 (32)

Study for Portrait of Van Gogh VI 1957 (33)

Figures in a Landscape 1956–7 (30)

Figure in Landscape (Miss Diana Watson) 1957 (34)

Miss Muriel Belcher 1959 (35)

Head of Woman 1960 (36)

Reclining Woman 1961 (37)

Study from Innocent X 1962 (38)

Landscape near Malabata, Tangier 1963 (41)

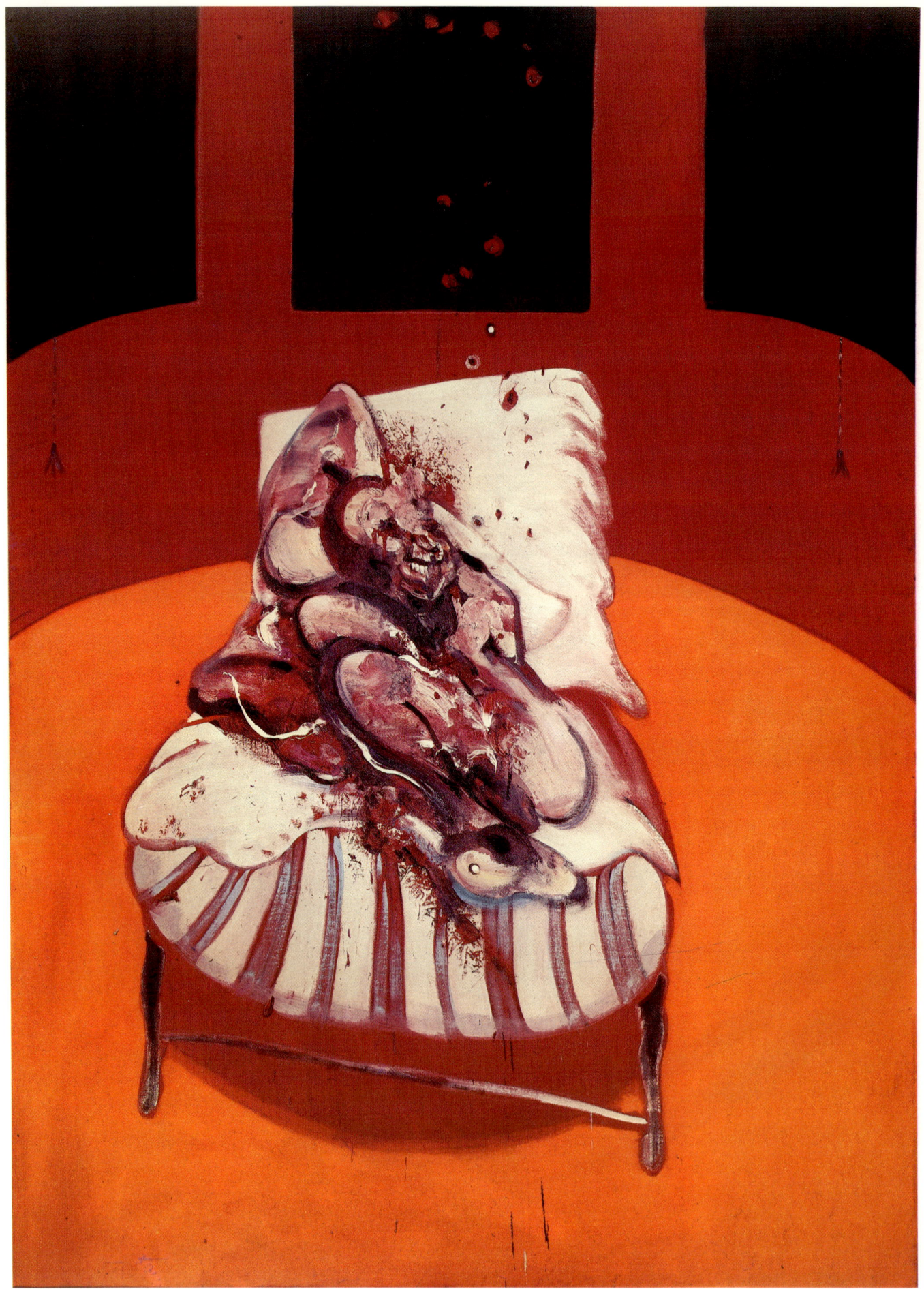

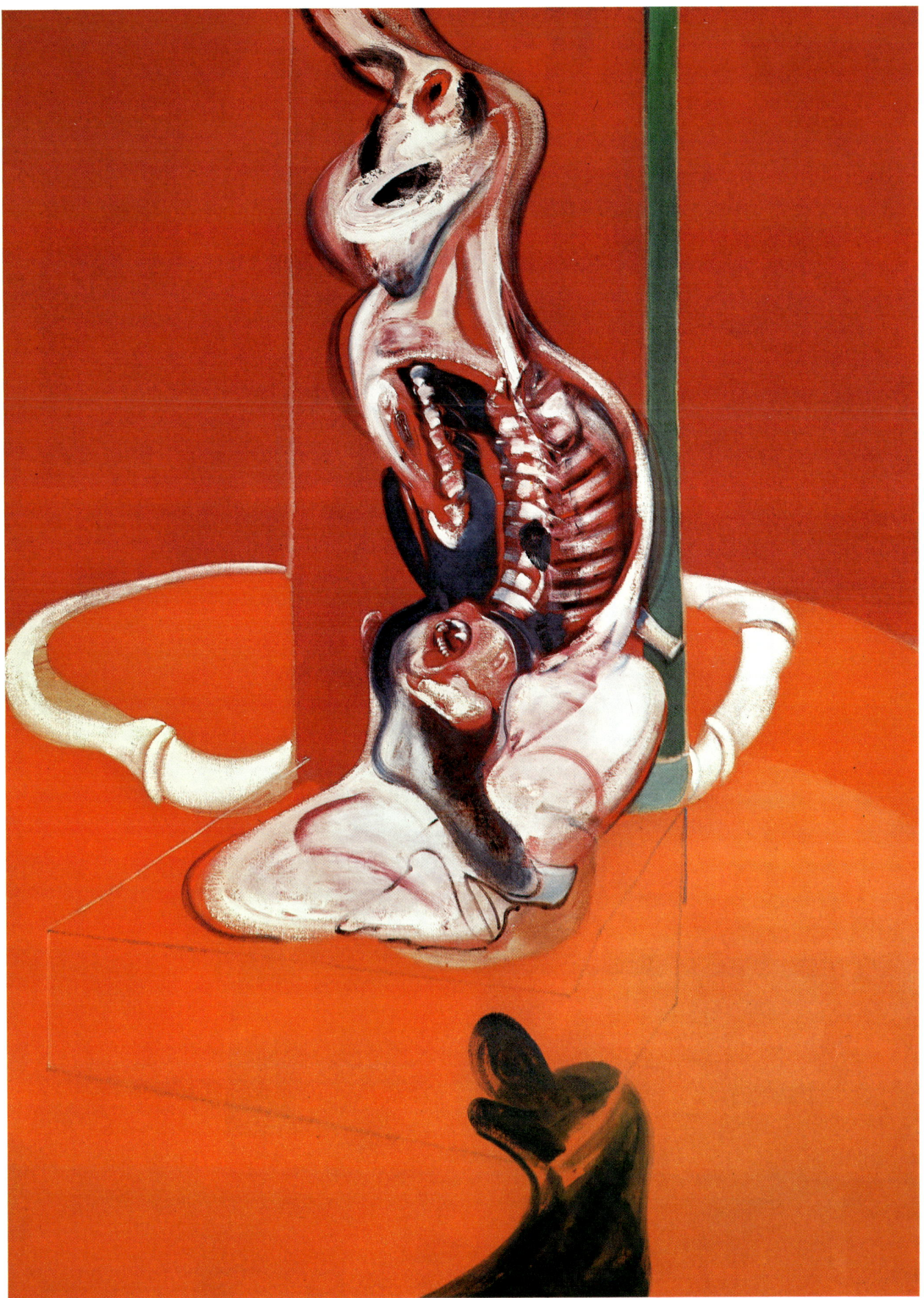

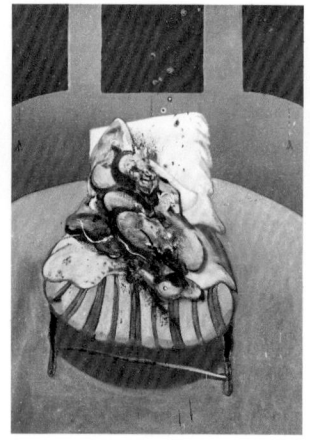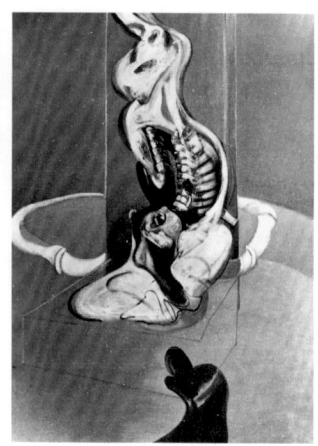

Three Studies for a Crucifixion 1962 (39)

Lying Figure with Hypodermic Syringe 1963 (40)

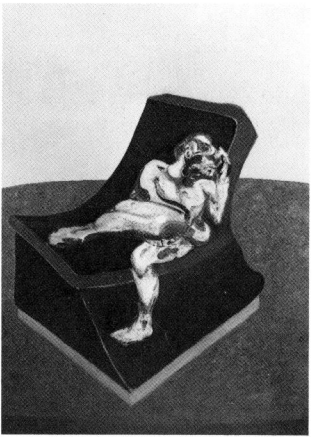

Three Figures in a Room 1964 (42)

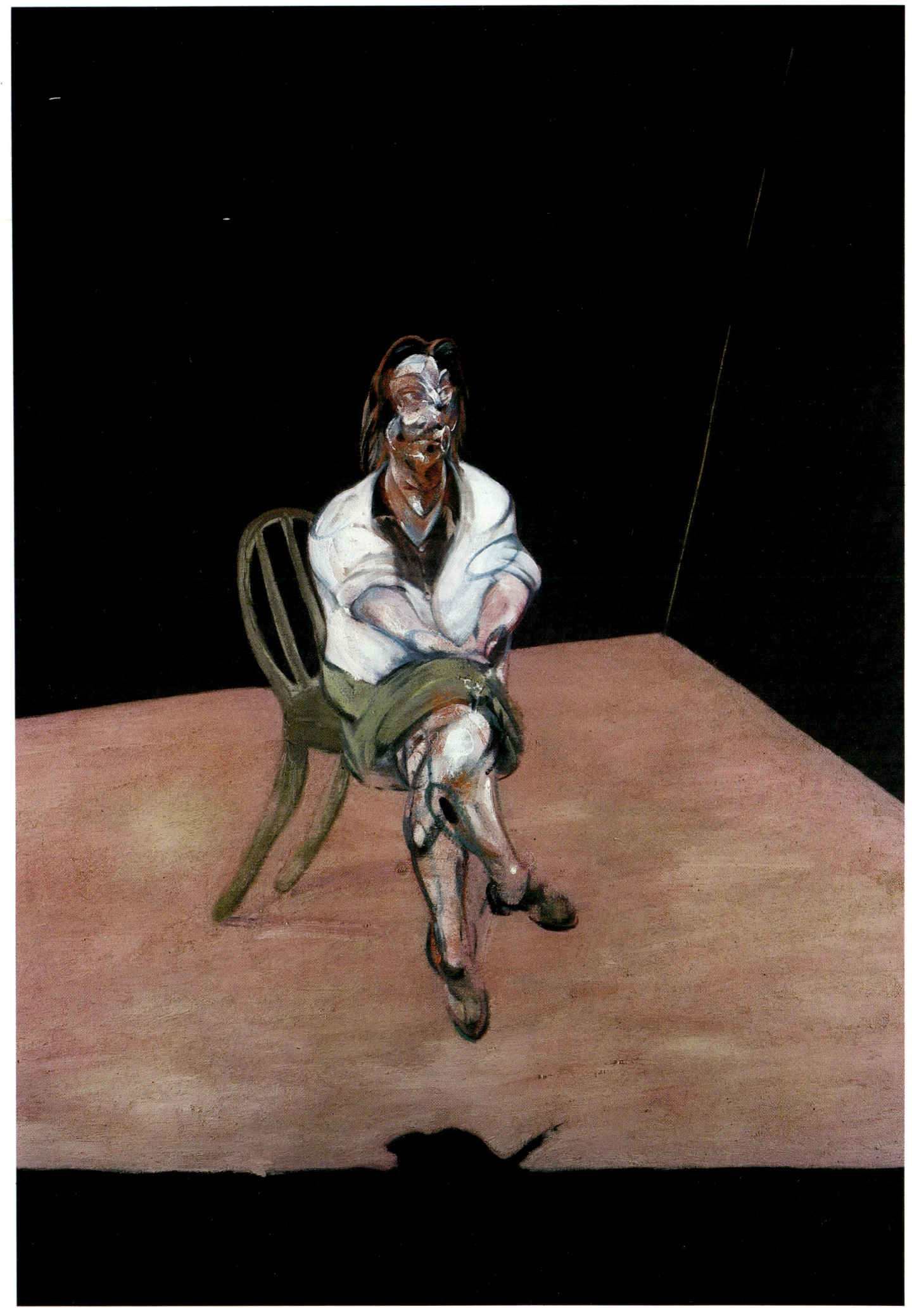

Study for Portrait (Isabel Rawsthorne) 1964 (43)

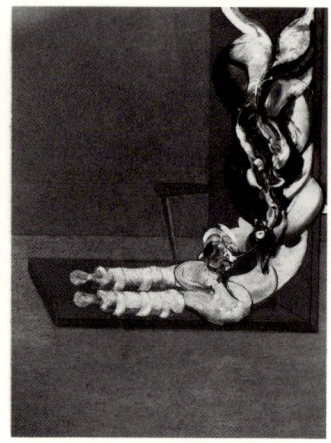

Crucifixion 1965 (45)

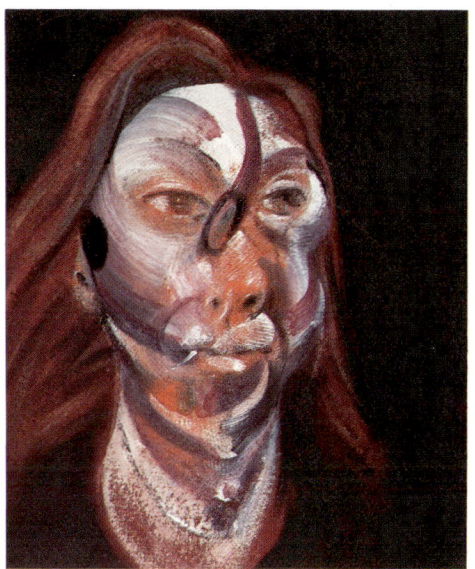

Three Studies for Head of Isabel Rawsthorne 1965 (44)

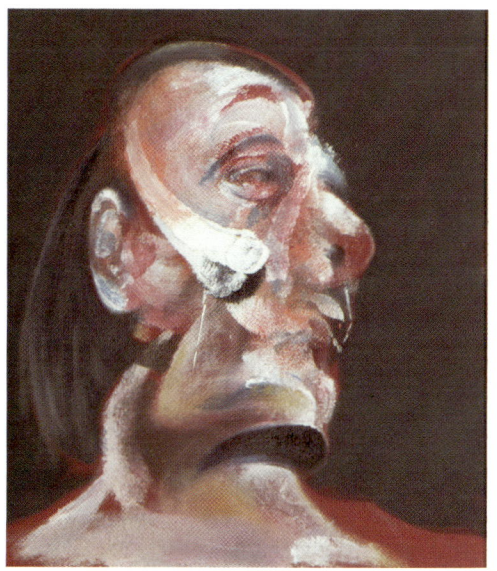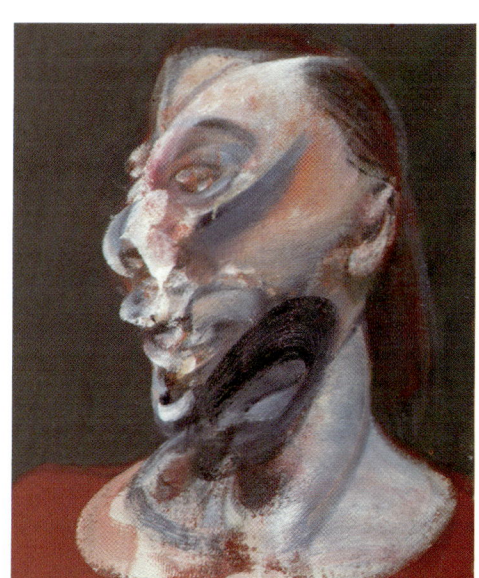

Three Studies of Muriel Belcher 1966 (50)

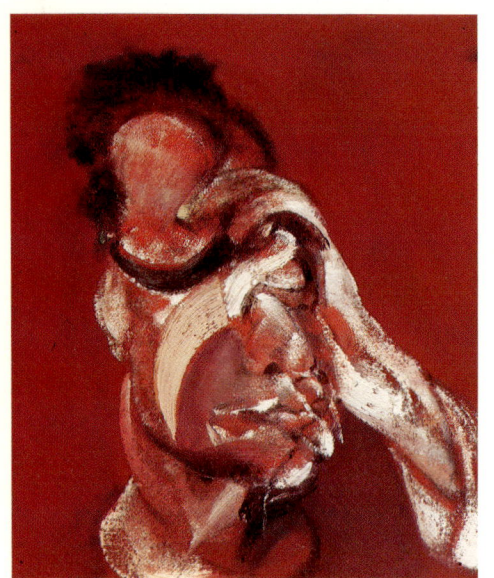

Three Studies for Portrait of Lucian Freud 1965 (47)

After Muybridge – Study of the Human Figure in Motion – Woman Emptying a Bowl of Water, and Paralytic Child on All Fours 1965 (46)

Portrait of Isabel Rawsthorne Standing in a Street in Soho 1967 (52)

Three Studies of Isabel Rawsthorne 1967 (54)

Study of Isabel Rawsthorne 1966 (48)

Portrait of George Dyer Riding a Bicycle 1966 (51)

Portrait of George Dyer Staring at a Blind-cord 1966 (49)

Portrait of George Dyer in a Mirror 1967–8 (55)

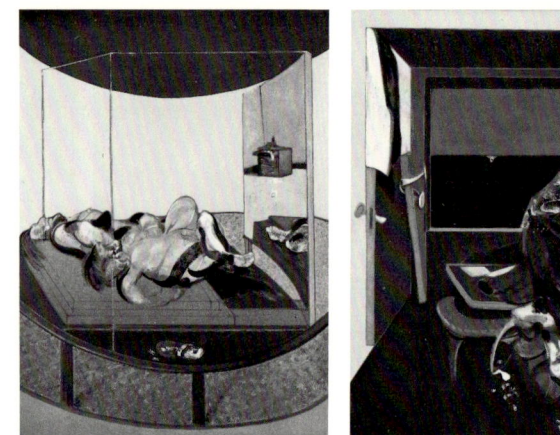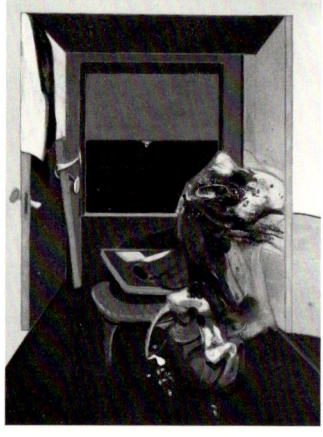

Triptych Inspired by T.S. Eliot's Poem 'Sweeney Agonistes' 1967 (53)

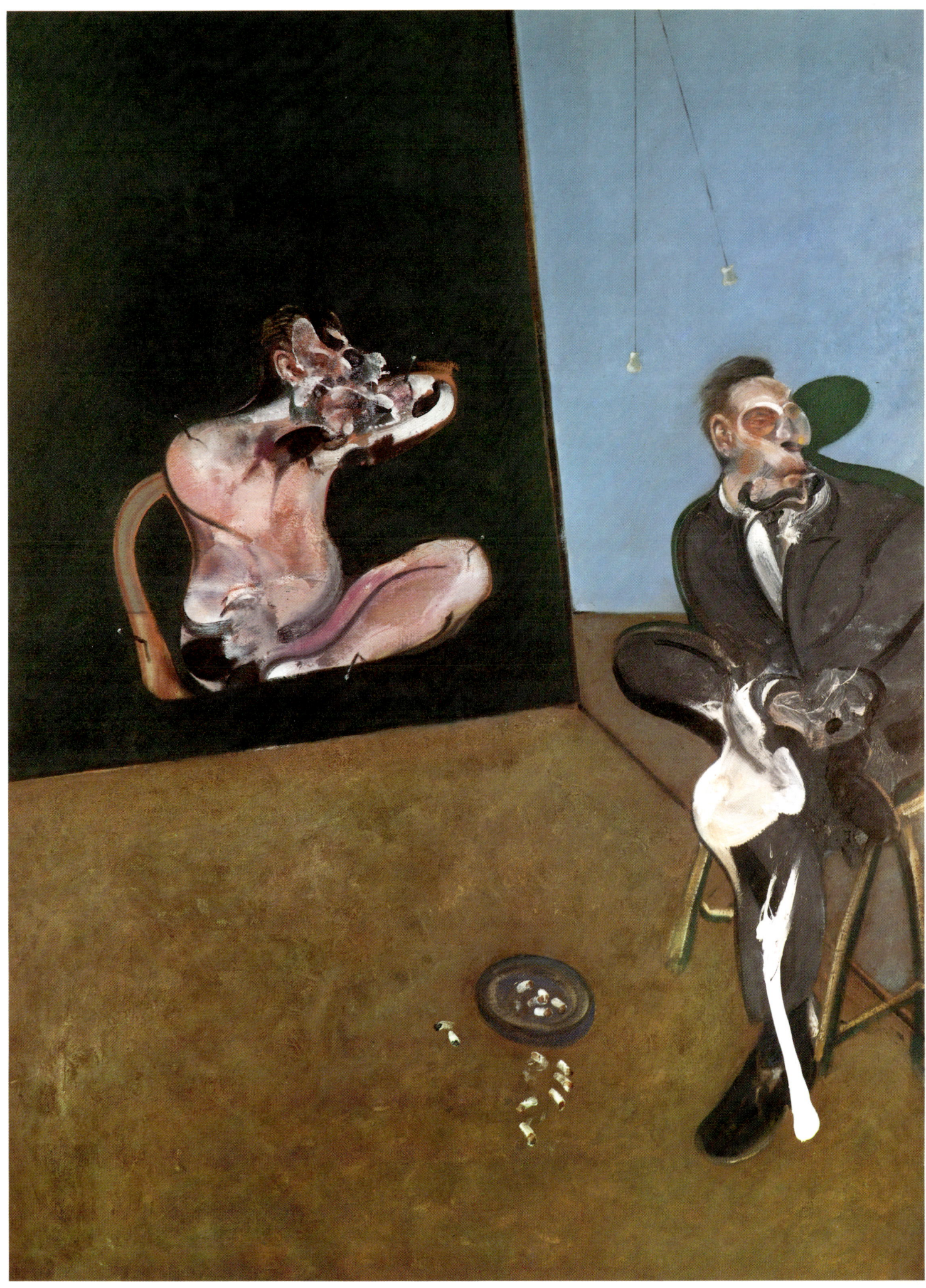

Two Studies for a Portrait of George Dyer 1968 (57)

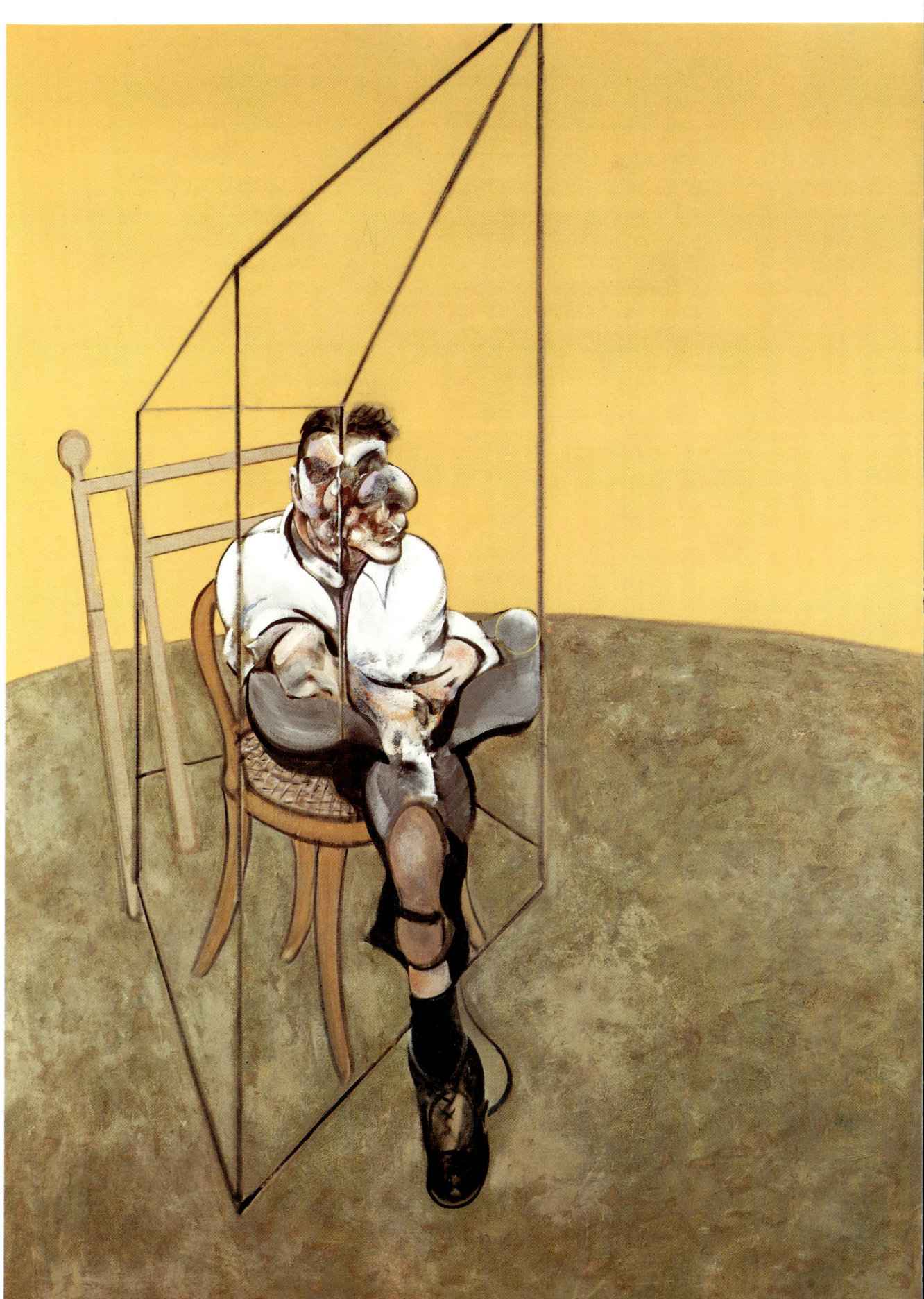

Triptych – Two Figures Lying on a Bed with Attendants 1968 (58)

Two Studies of George Dyer with Dog 1968 (56)

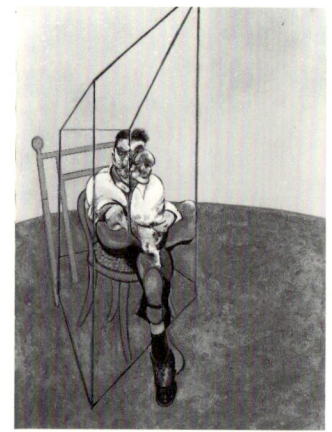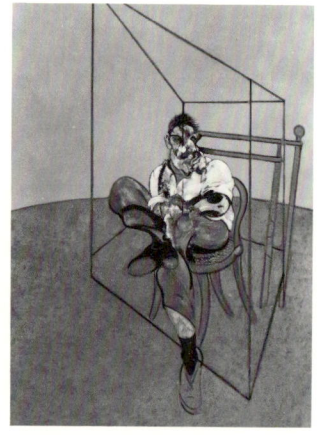

Three Studies of Lucian Freud 1969 (59)

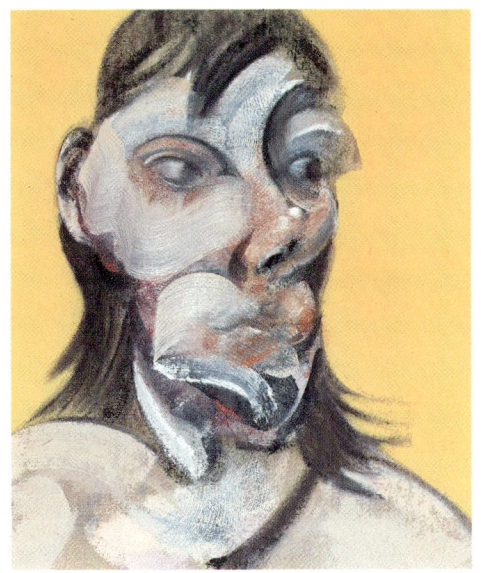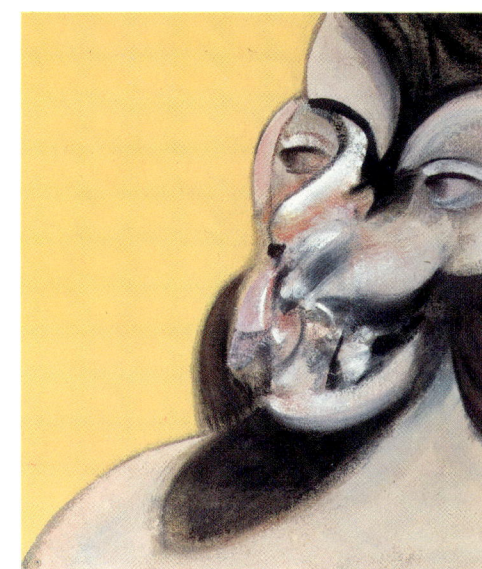

Three Studies of Henrietta Moraes 1969 (63)

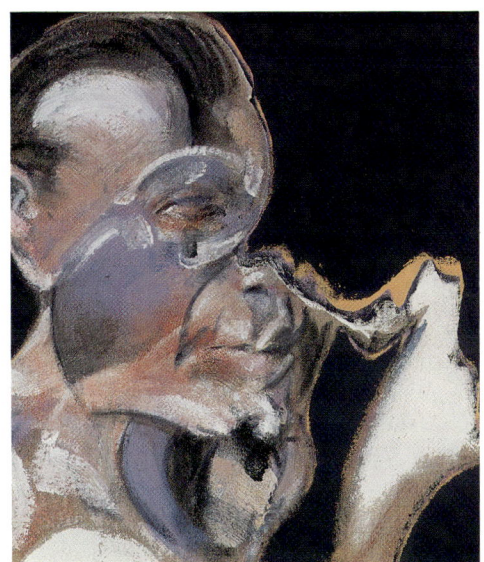

Three Studies for Portraits Including Self Portrait 1969 (64)

Lying Figure 1969 (61)

Studies of George Dyer and Isabel Rawsthorne 1970 (70)

Study for Bullfight No. 1 1969 (60)

Second Version of Study for Bullfight No. 1 1969 (62)

Study of Nude with Figure in a Mirror 1969 (65)

Study of Henrietta Moraes 1969 (67)

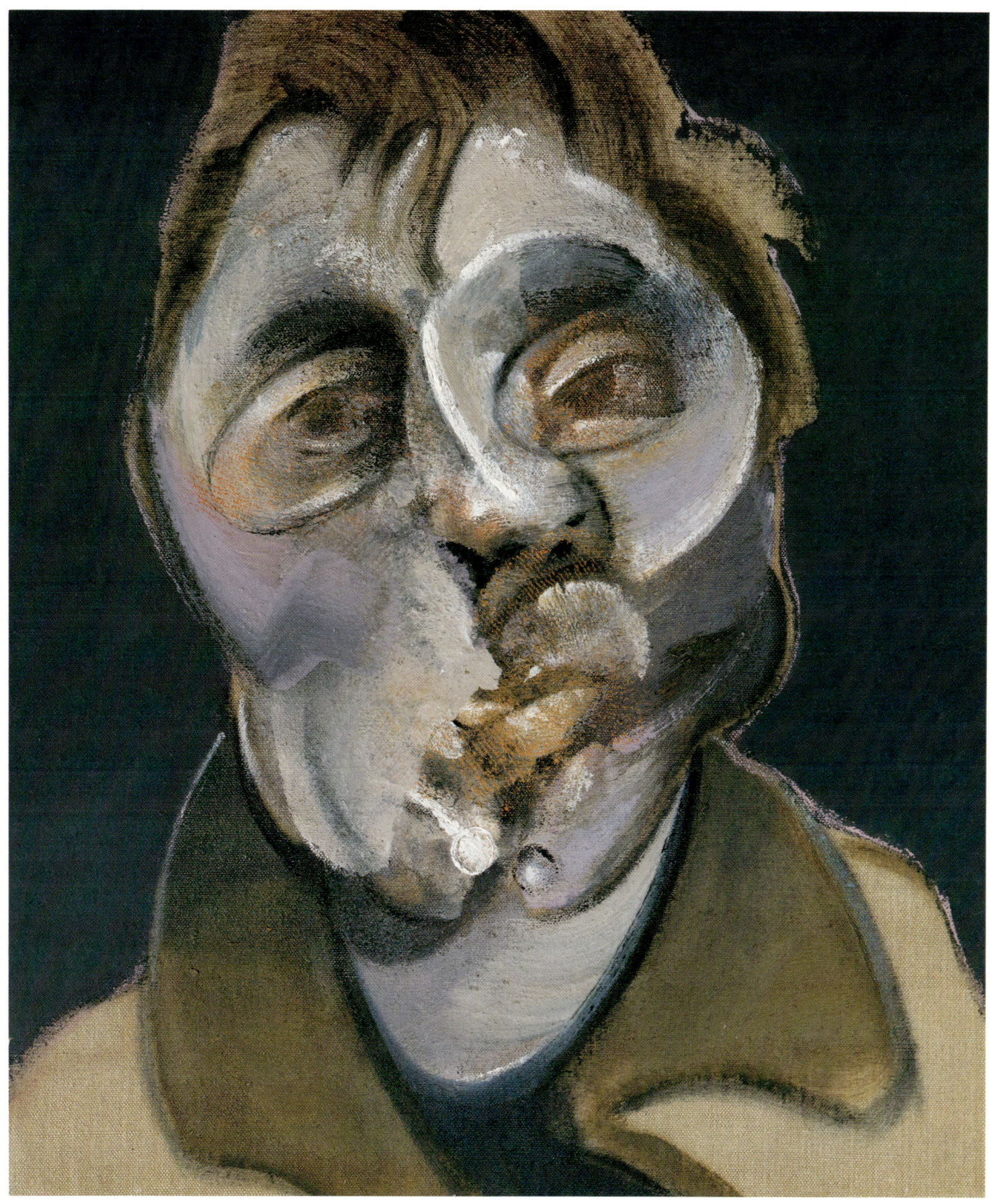

Self Portrait 1969 (66)

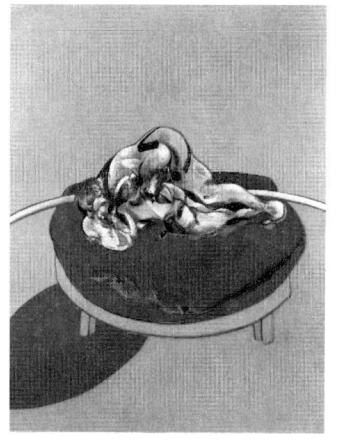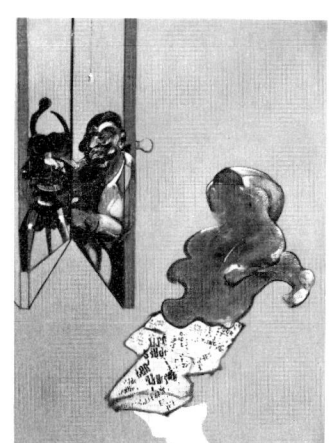

Triptych – Studies from the Human Body 1970 (69)

Self Portrait 1970 (72)

Study for Portrait 1970 (68)

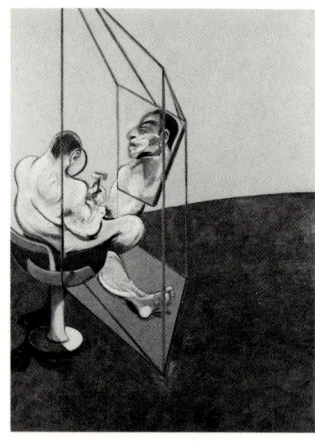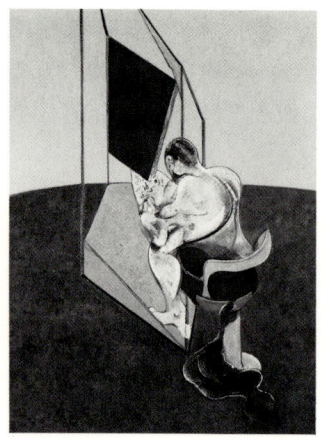

Three Studies of the Male Back 1970 (71)

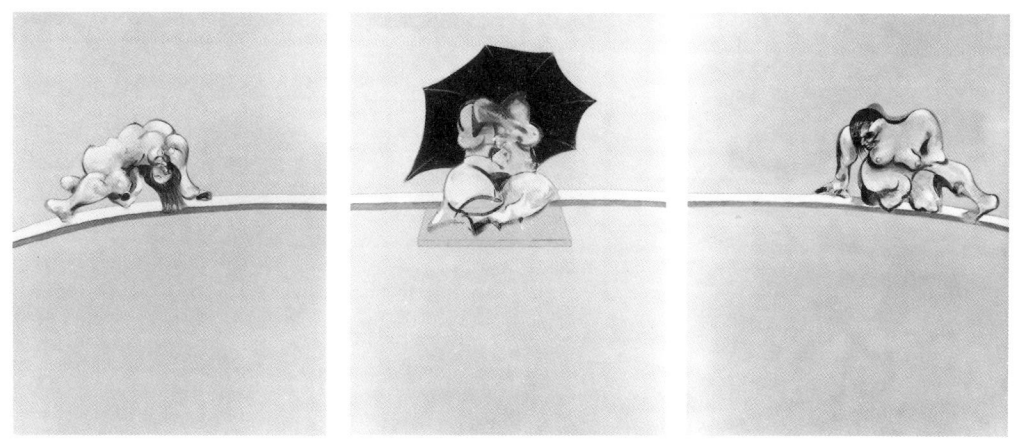

Triptych – Studies of the Human Body 1970 (73)

Triptych 1971 (77)

Second Version of 'Painting 1946' 1971 (74)

Second Version of 'Painting 1946' 1971 (74)

Study for Portrait of Lucian Freud (Sideways) August 1971 (76)

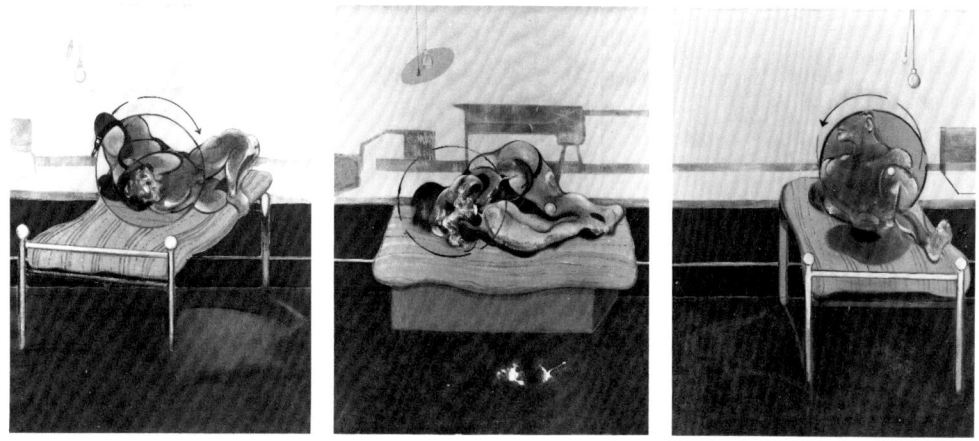

Three Studies of Figures on Beds 1972 (78)

Triptych August 1972 (81)

Self Portrait 1971 (75)

Self Portrait 1972 (79)

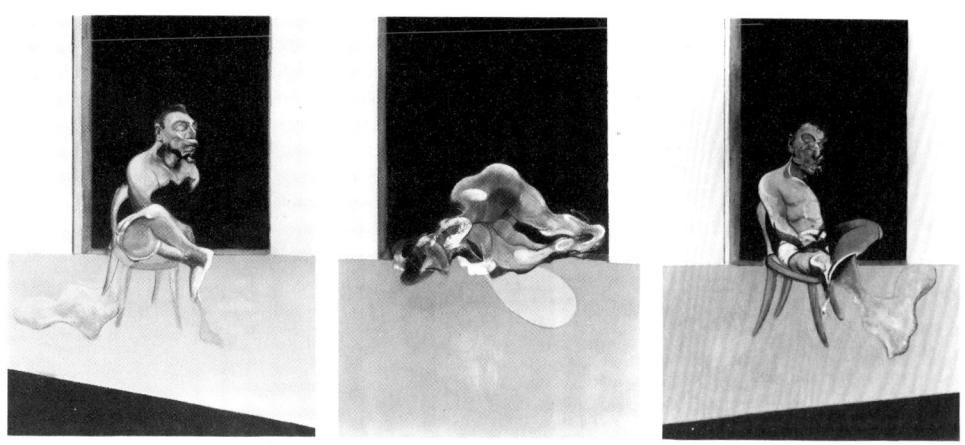

Triptych August 1972 (81)

Self Portrait 1971 (75)

Self Portrait 1972 (79)

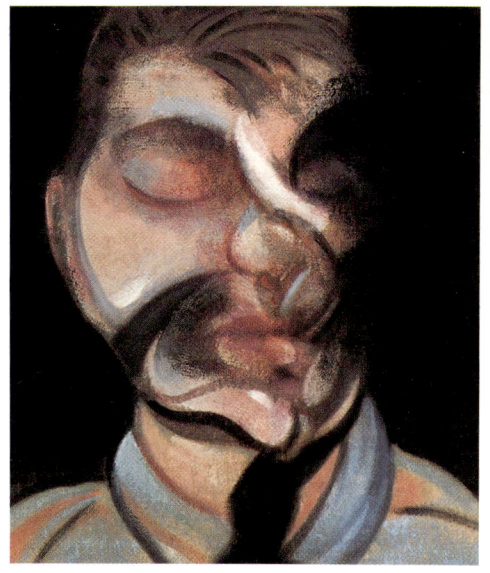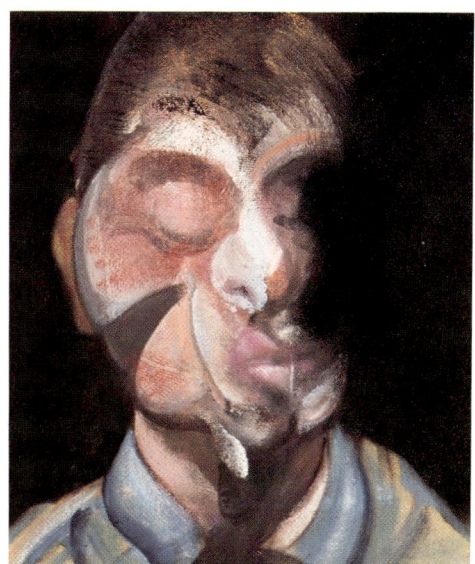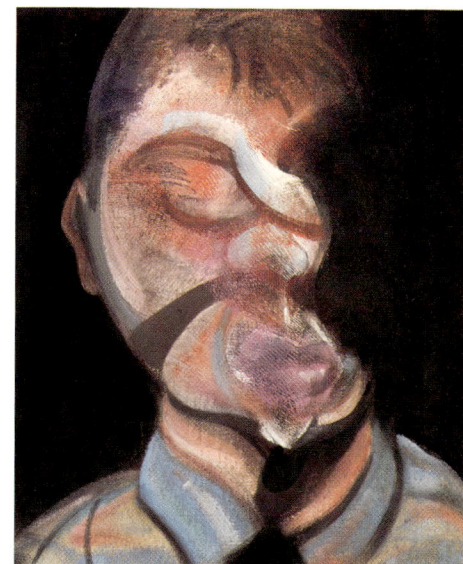

Three Studies for Self Portrait 1972 (80)

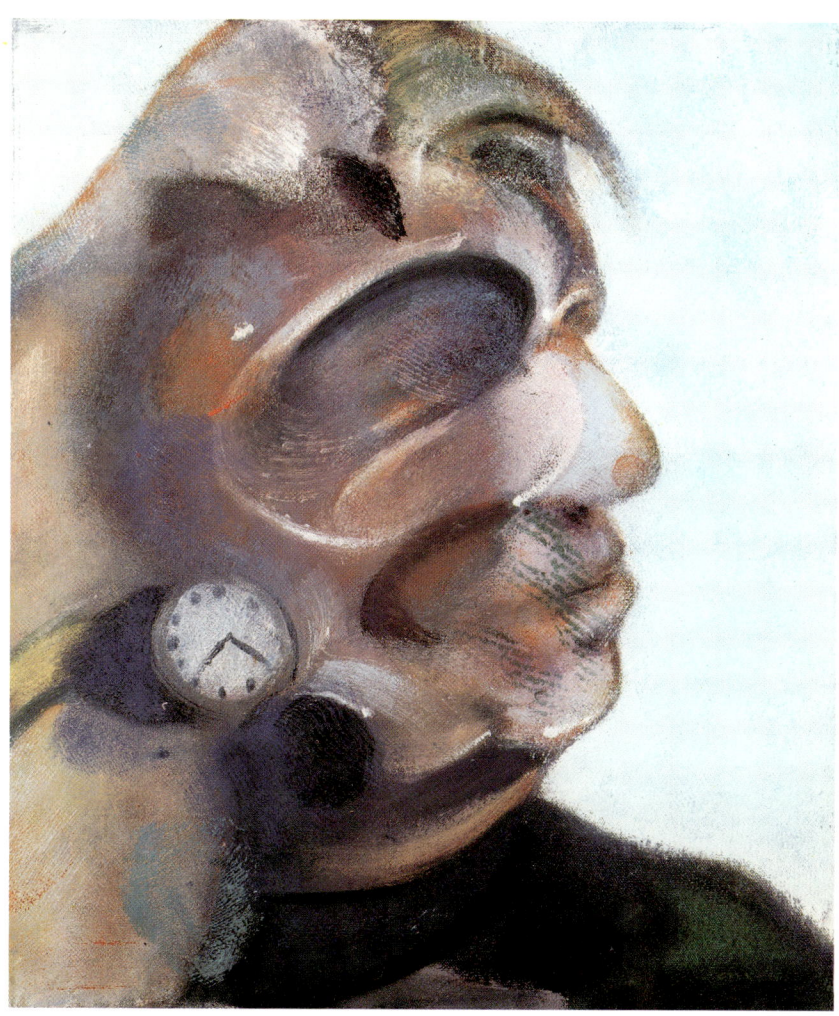

Study for Self Portrait 1973 (83)

Self Portrait 1973 (84)

Self Portrait 1973 (86)

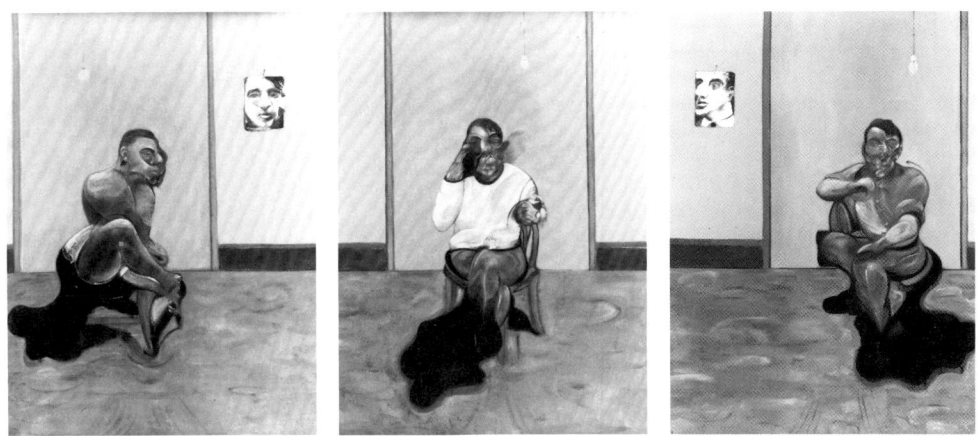

Three Portraits: Posthumous Portrait of George Dyer,
Self Portrait, Portrait of Lucian Freud 1973 (82)

Triptych May–June 1973 (85)

Seated Figure 1974 (89)

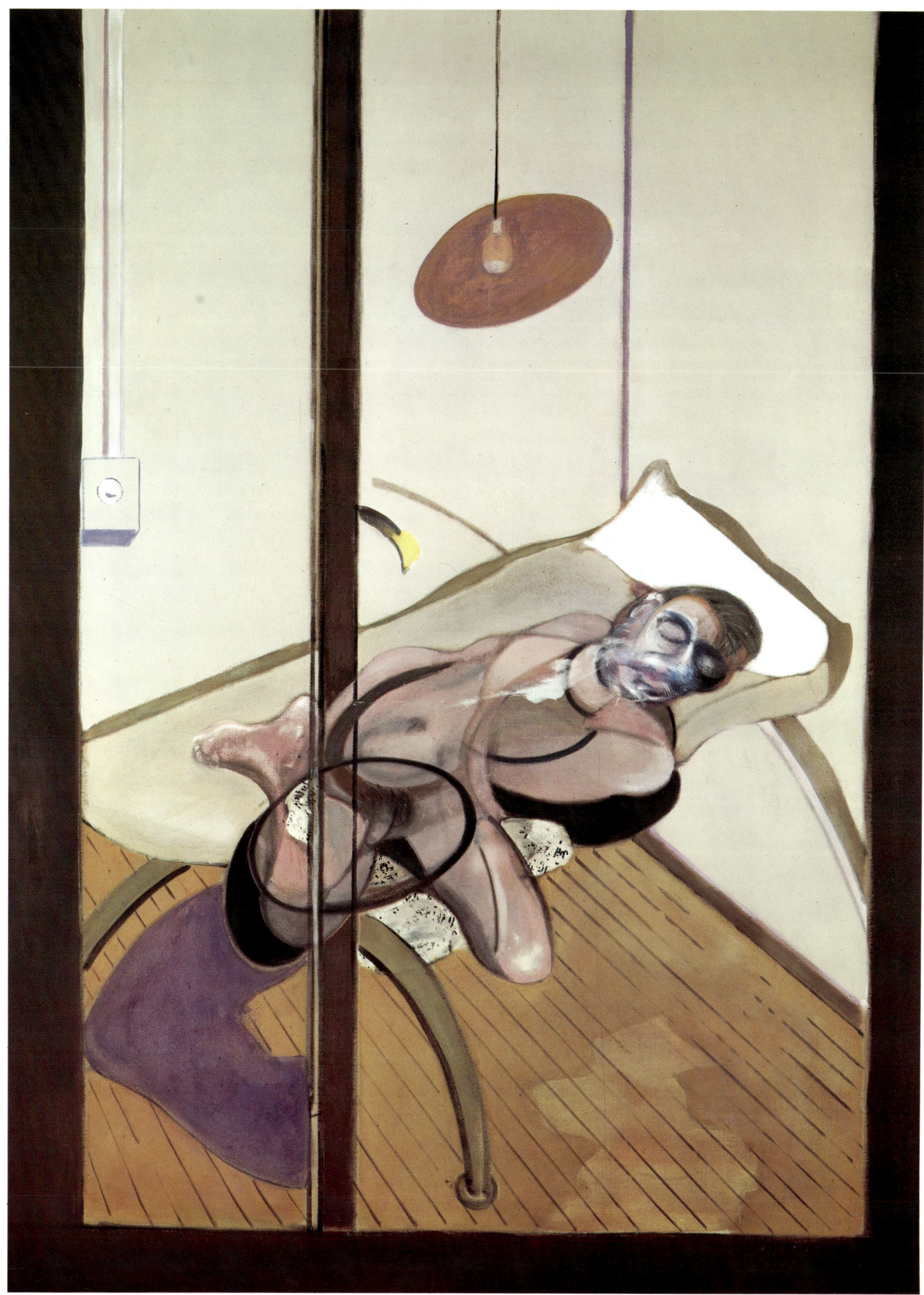

Sleeping Figure 1974 (88)

Study for a Human Body (Man Turning on the Light) 1973–4 (90)

Triptych March 1974 (87)

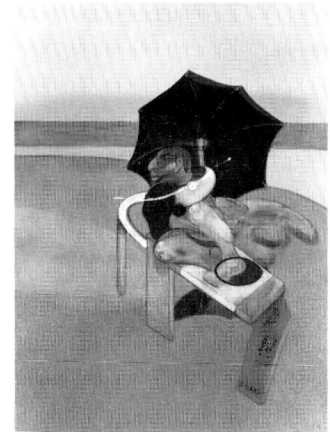

Triptych 1974–7 (101)

Portrait of a Dwarf 1975 (93)

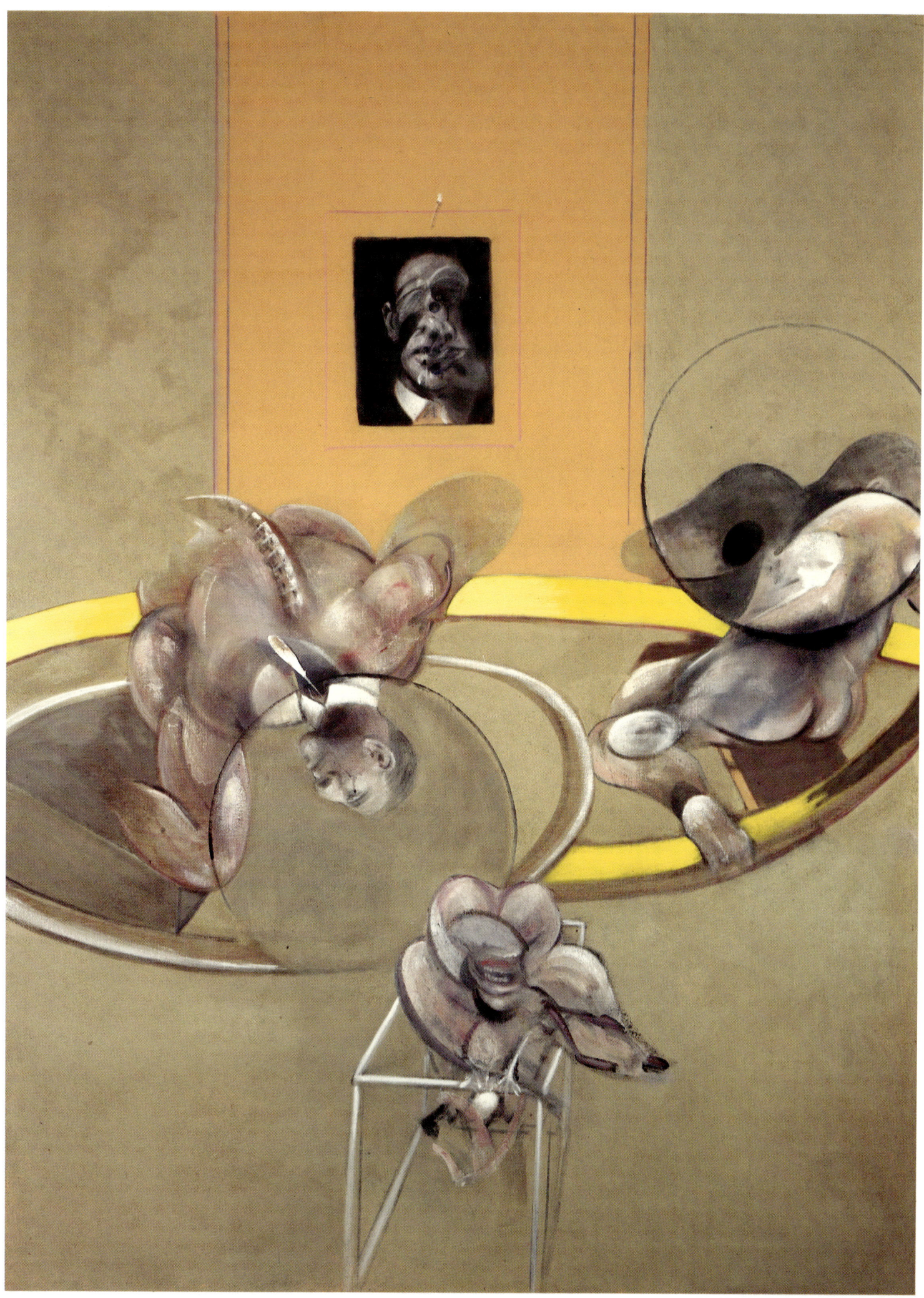

Three Figures and a Portrait 1975 (94)

Figure in Movement 1976 (Figur in Bewegung 1976) (96)

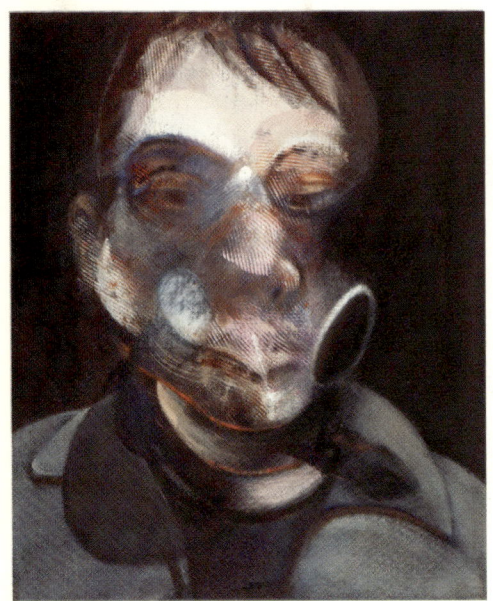 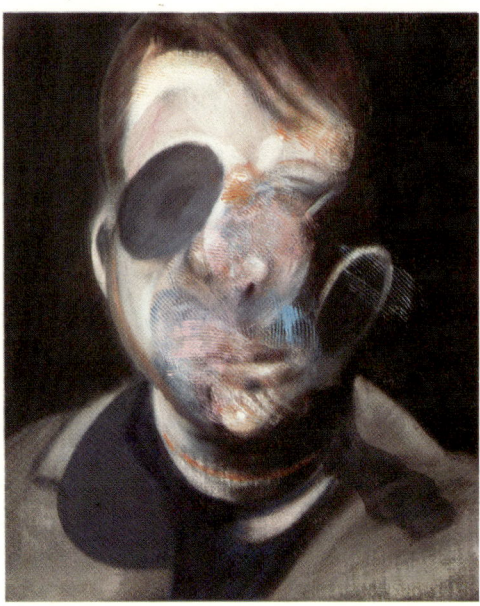 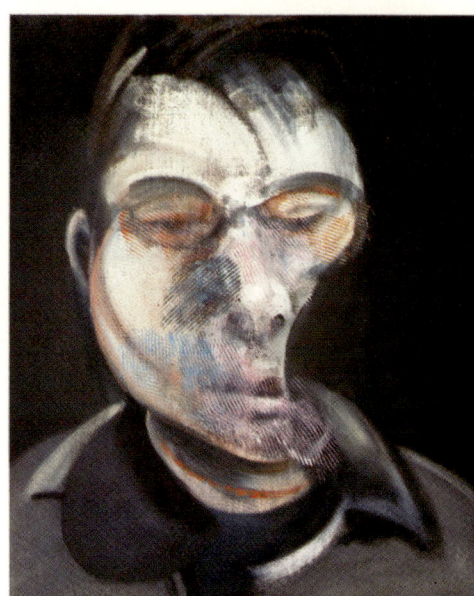

Three Studies for Self Portrait 1976 (Drei Studien für Selbstporträt 1976) (100)

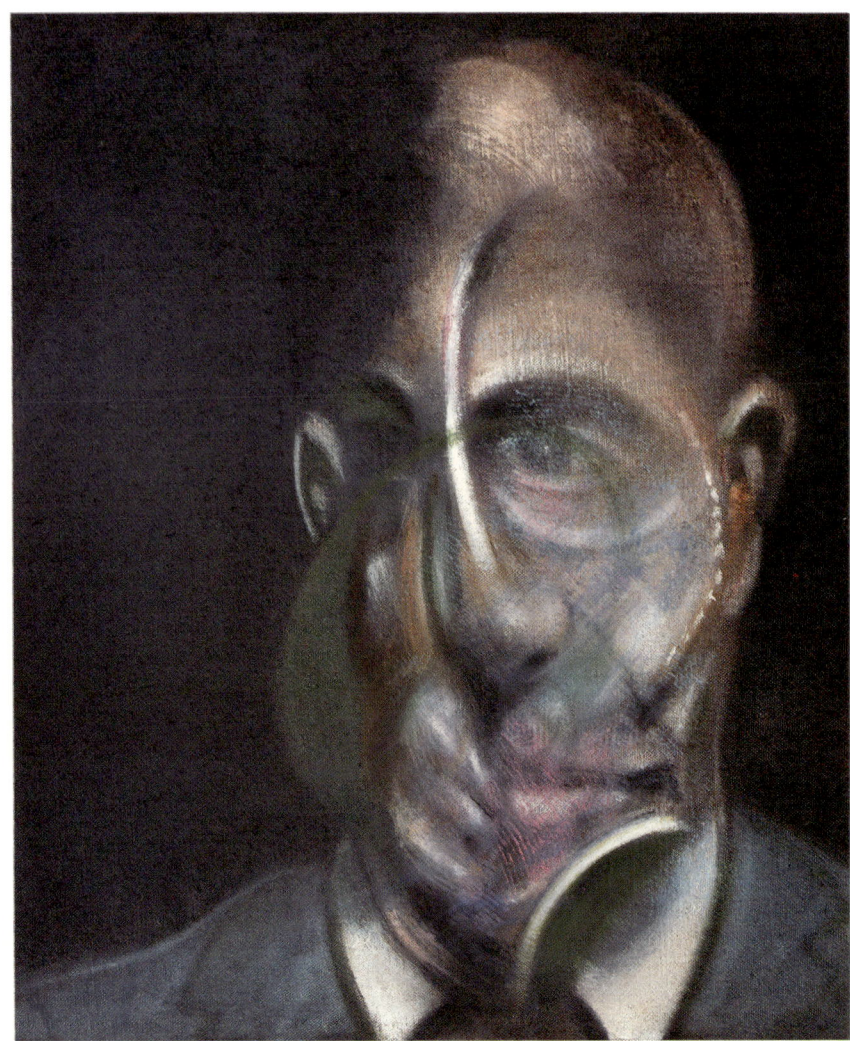

Portrait of Michel Leiris 1976 (Porträt Michel Leiris 1976) (97)

Studies from the Human Body 1975 (Studien nach dem menschlichen Körper 1975) (95)

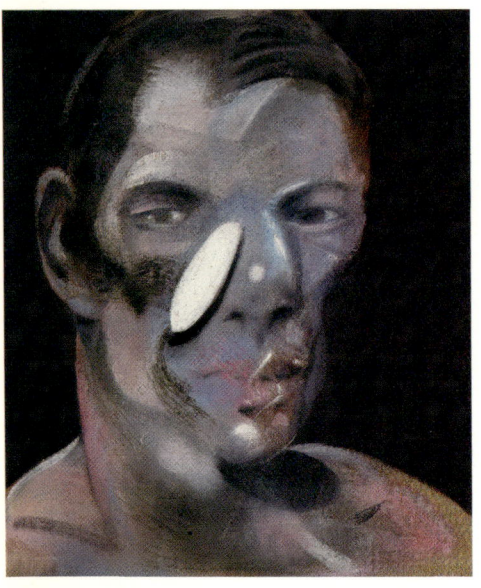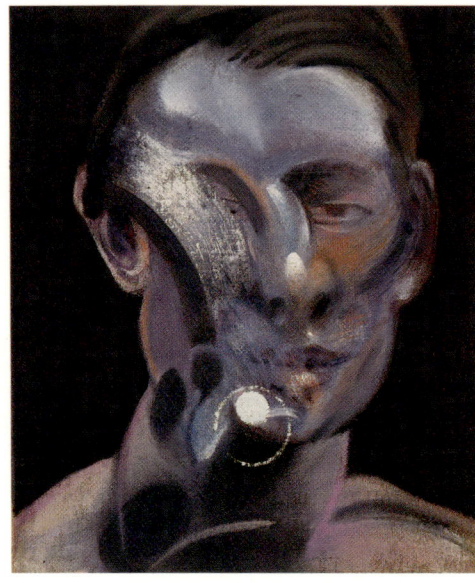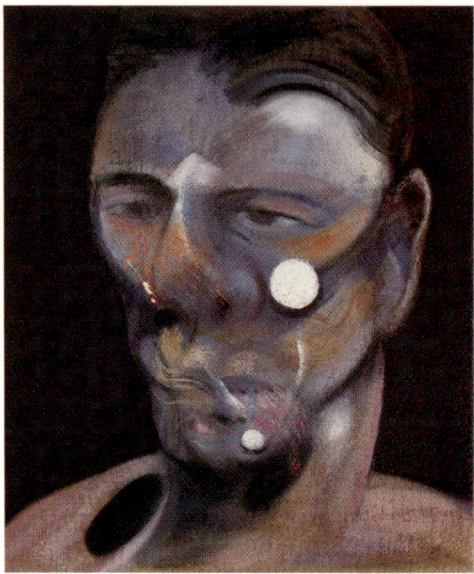

Three Studies for a Portrait of Peter Beard 1975 (Drei Studien für ein Porträt Peter Beard 1975) (91)

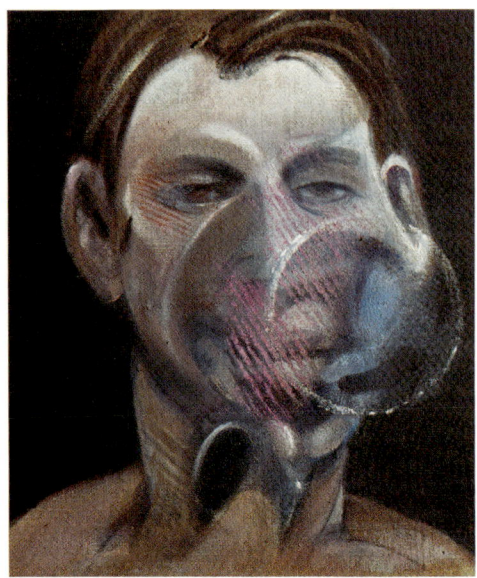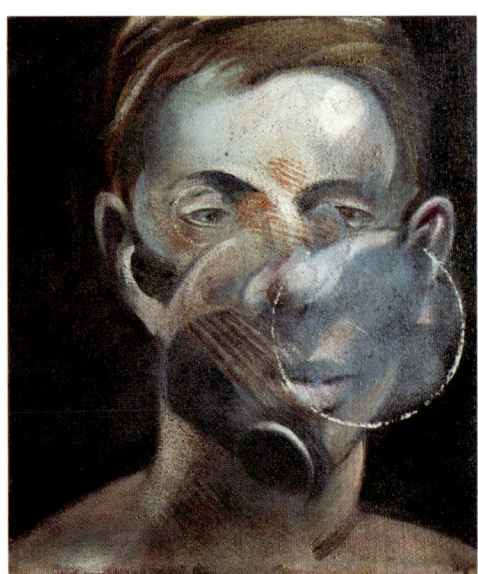

Three Studies for a Portrait (Peter Beard) 1975 (Drei Studien für ein Porträt – Peter Beard 1975) (92)

Figure Writing Reflected in a Mirror 1976 (99)

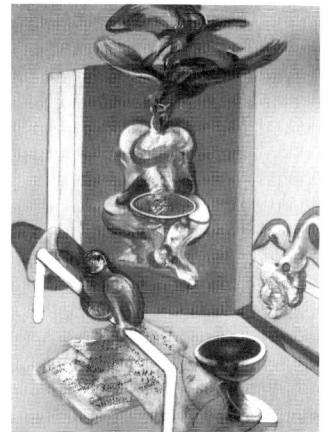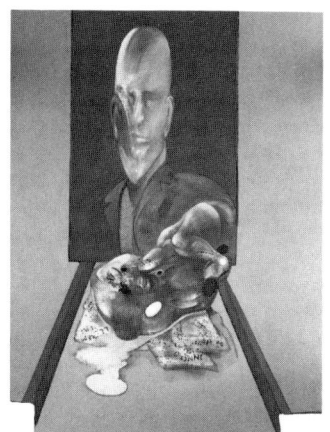

Triptych 1976 (98)

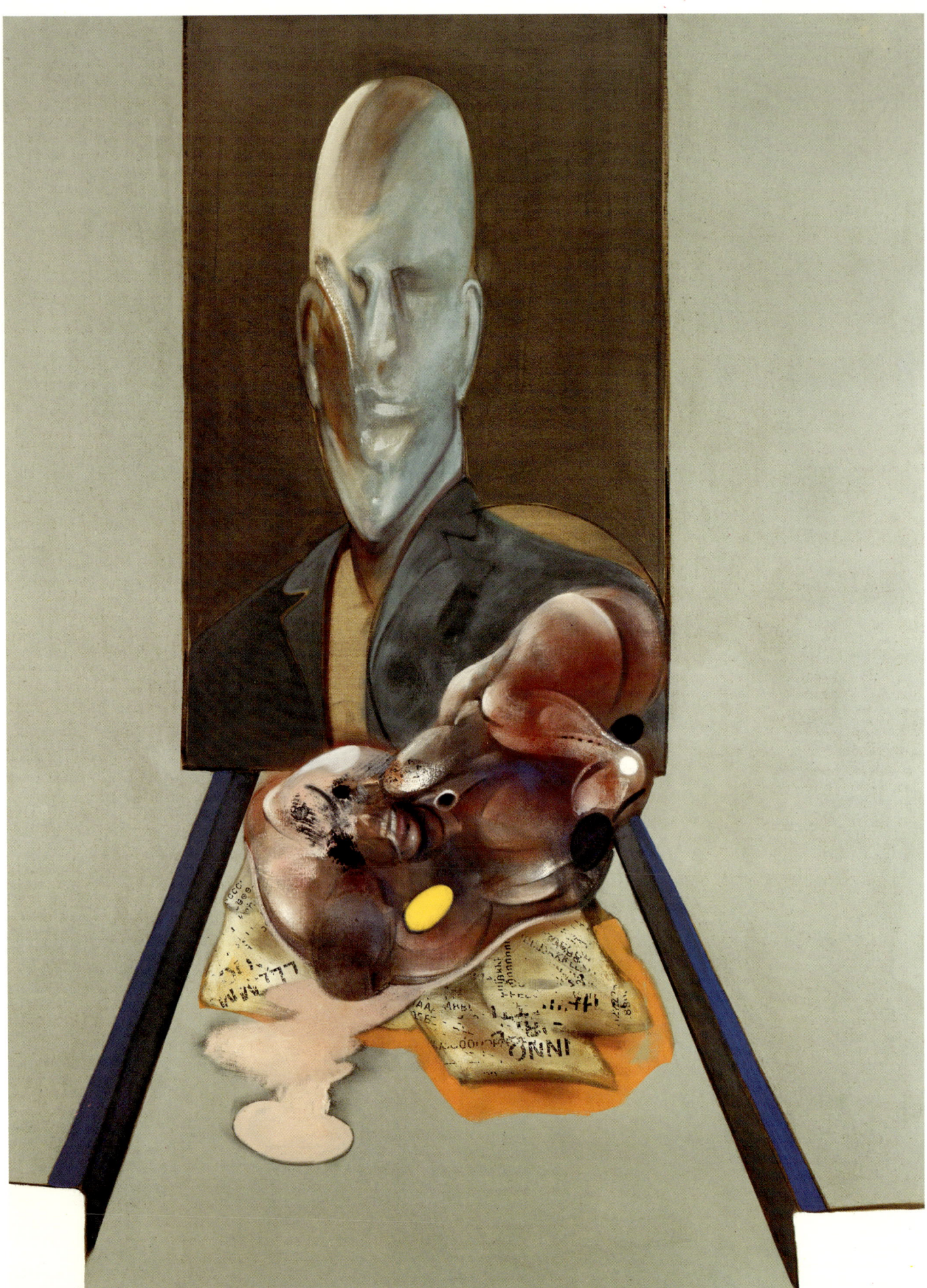

Figure in Movement 1978 (105)

Painting 1978 (Gemälde 1978) (104)

Landscape 1978 (Landschaft 1978) (103)

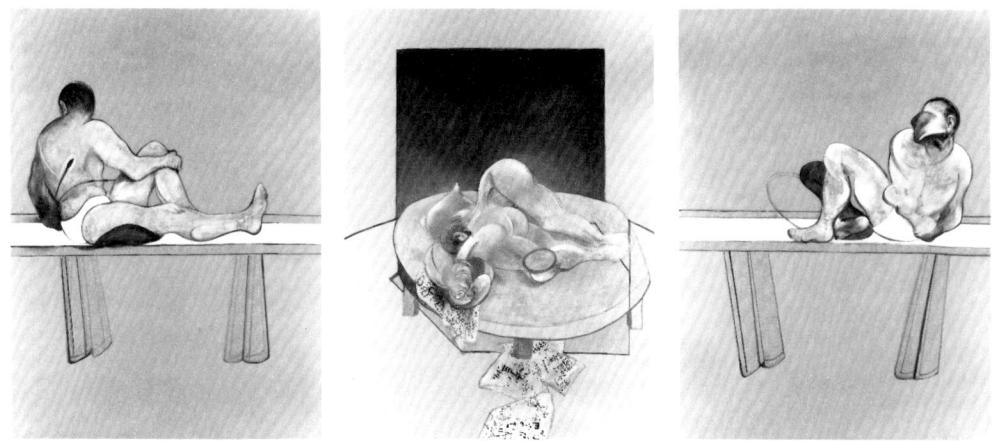

Triptych – Studies of the Human Body 1979 (107)

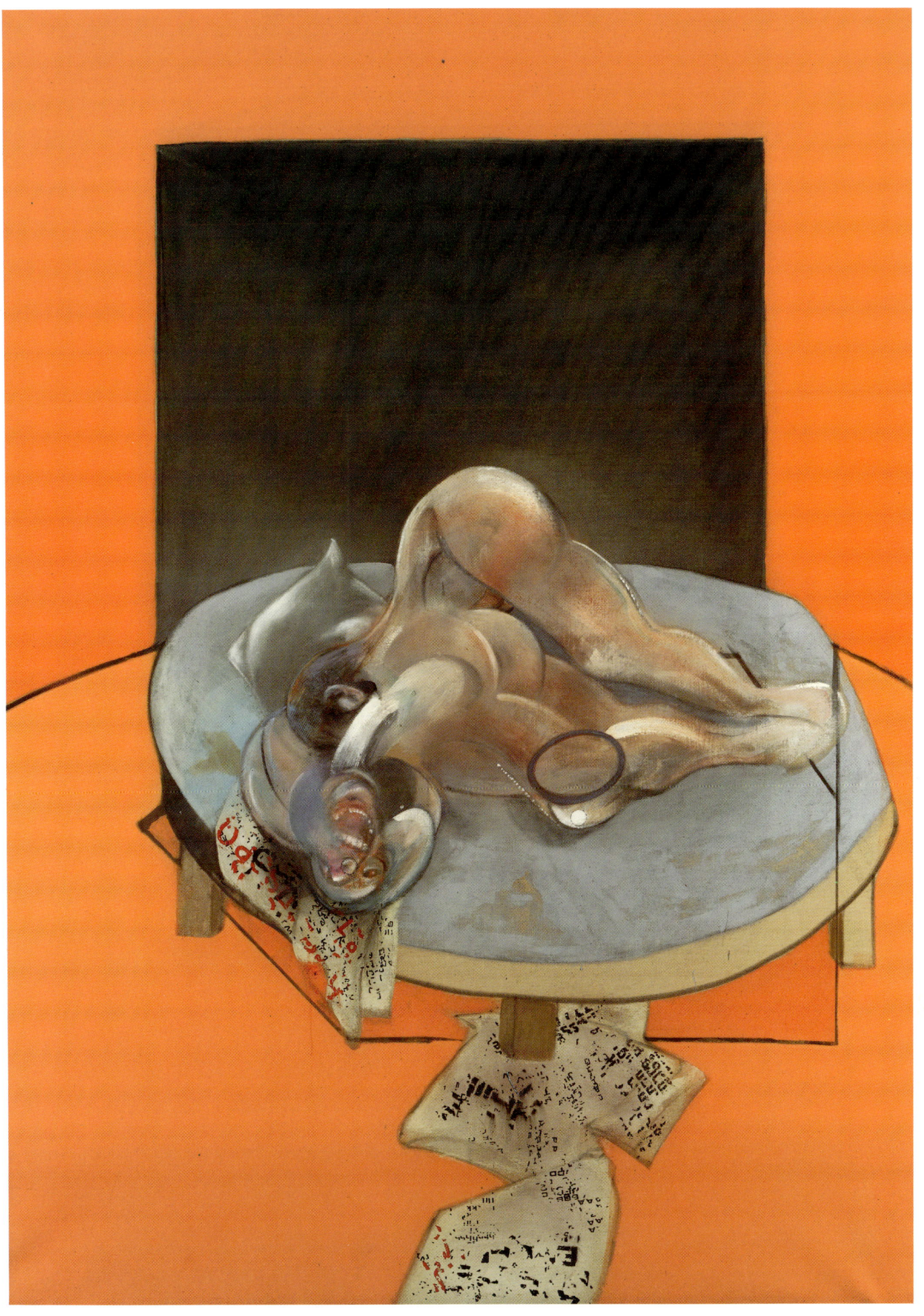

Study for Portrait (Michel Leiris) 1978 (102)

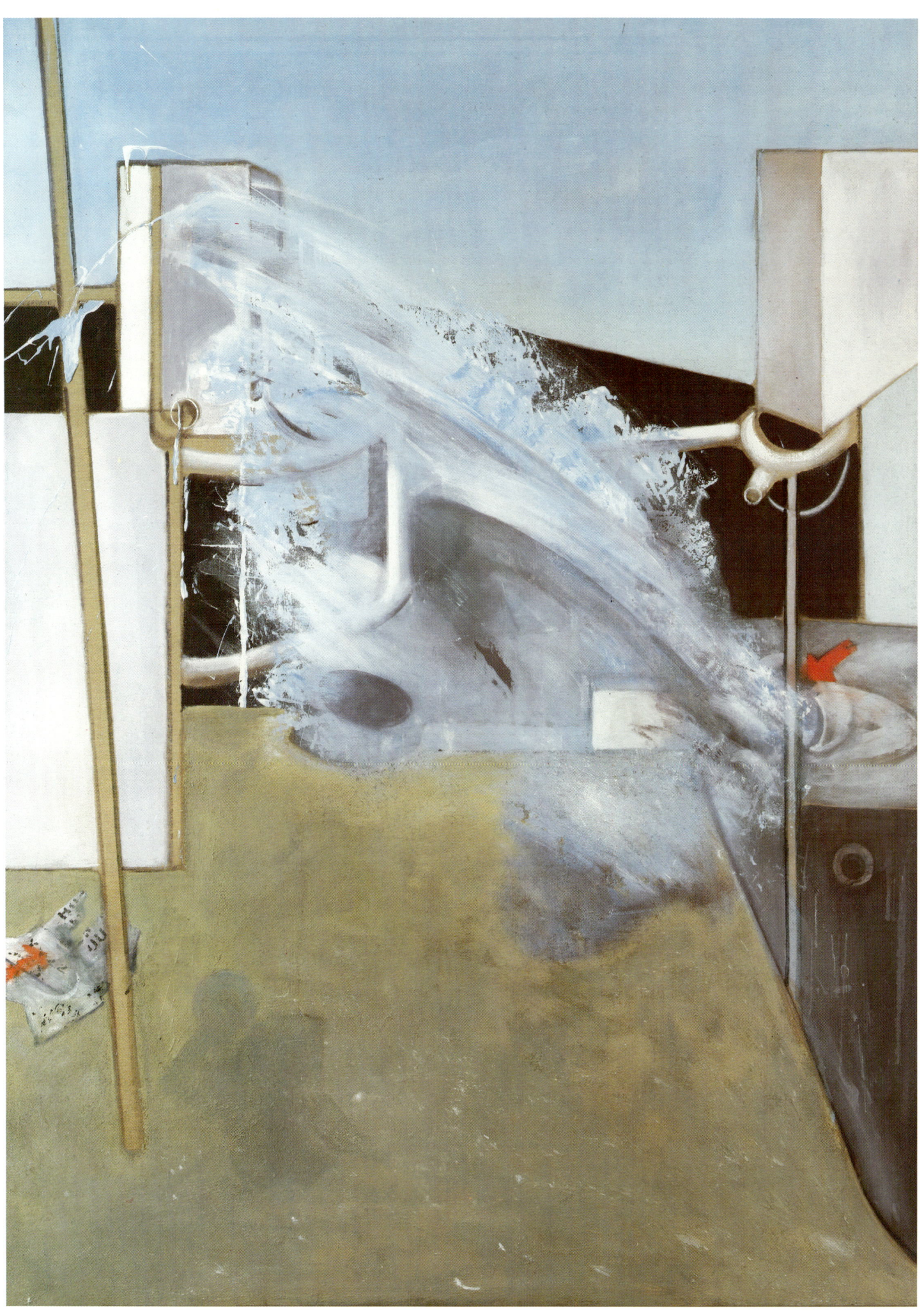

Jet of Water 1979 (106)

Three Studies for Self Portrait 1979 (109)

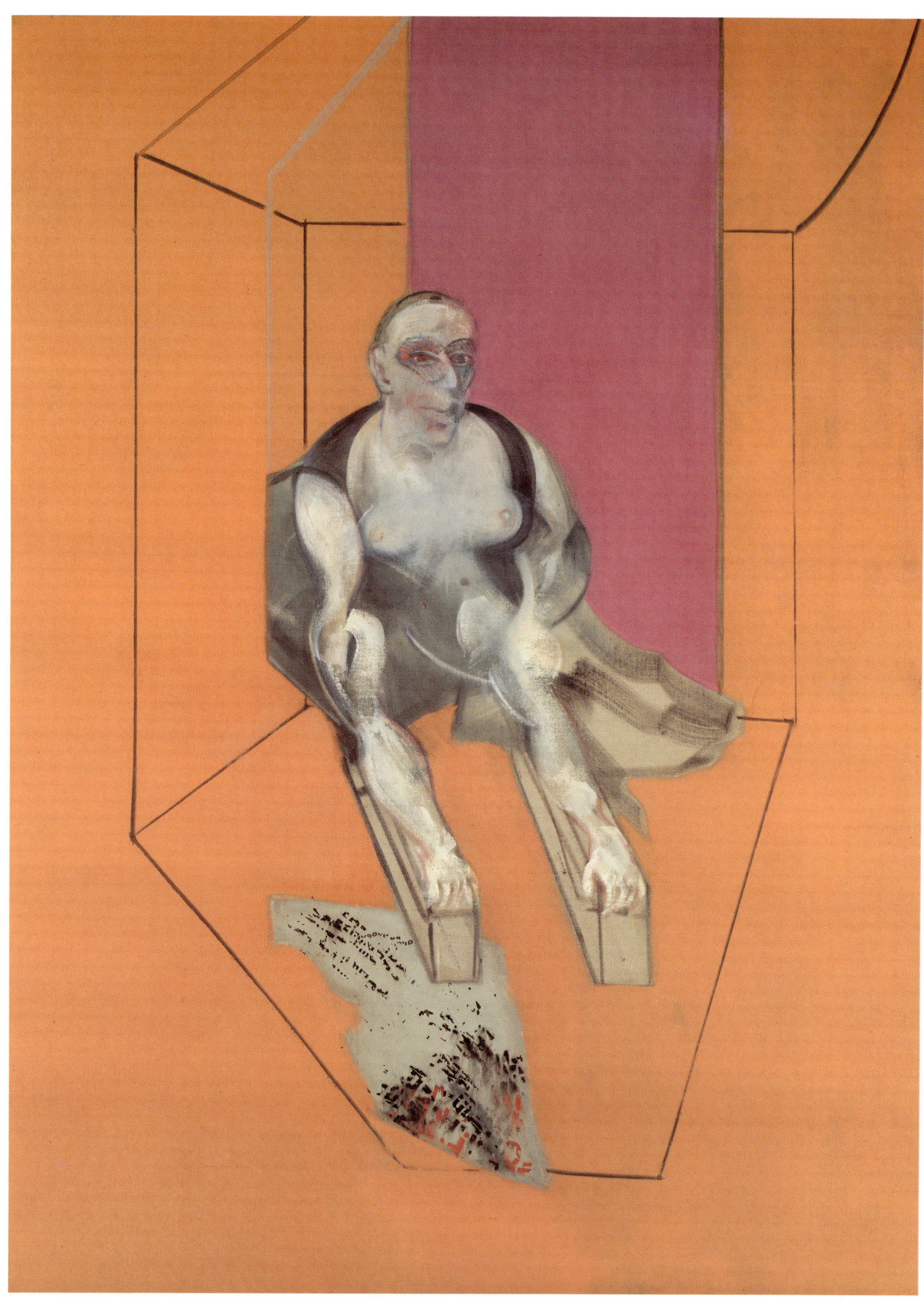

Sphinx – Portrait of Muriel Belcher 1979 (108)

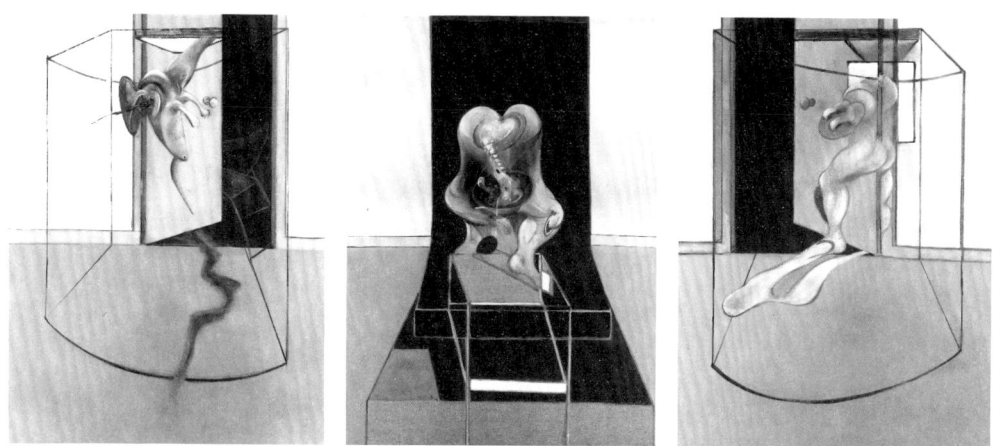

Triptych Inspired by the Oresteia of Aeschylus 1981 (110)

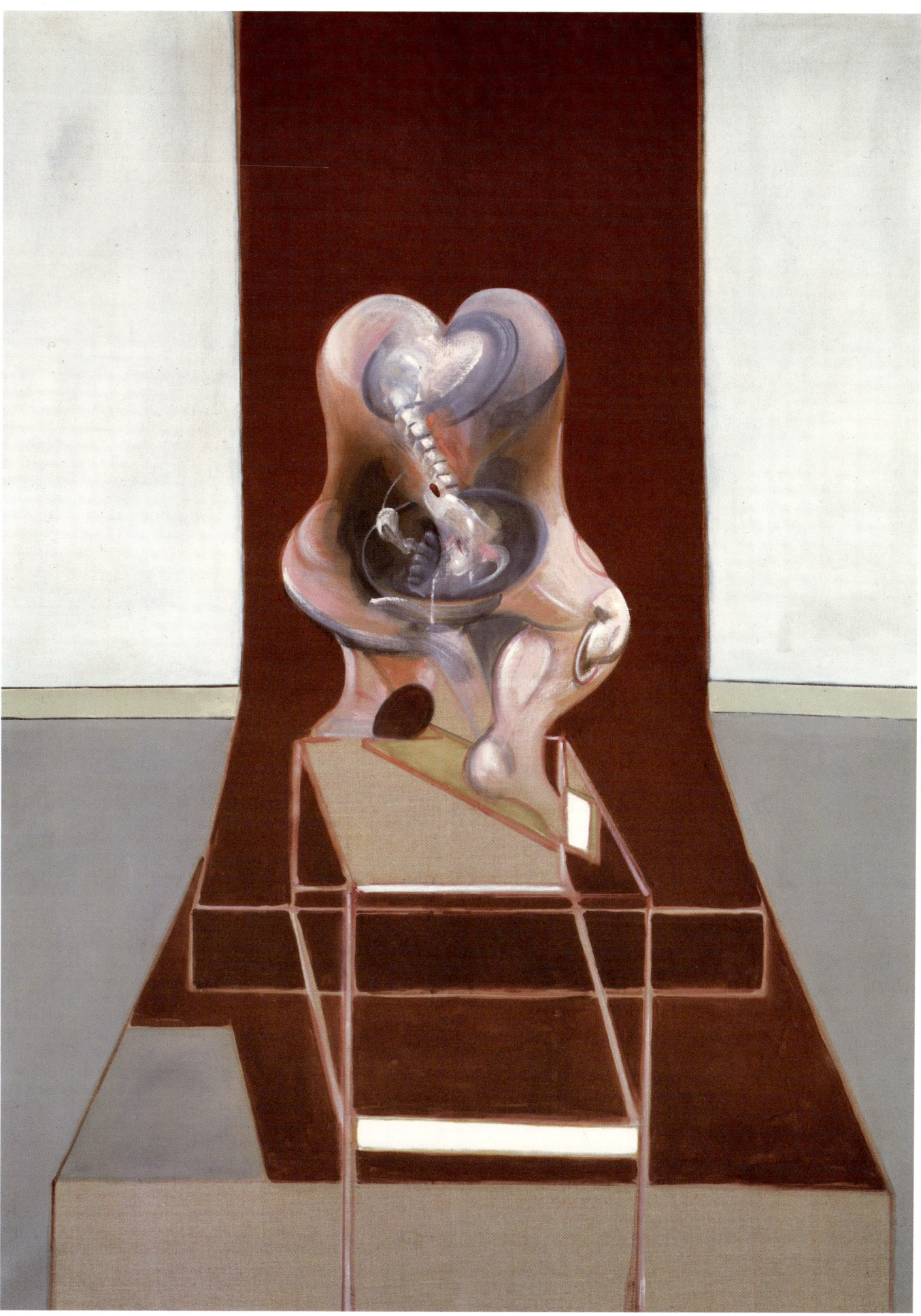

Sand Dune 1981 (111)

Water from a Running Tap 1982 (114)

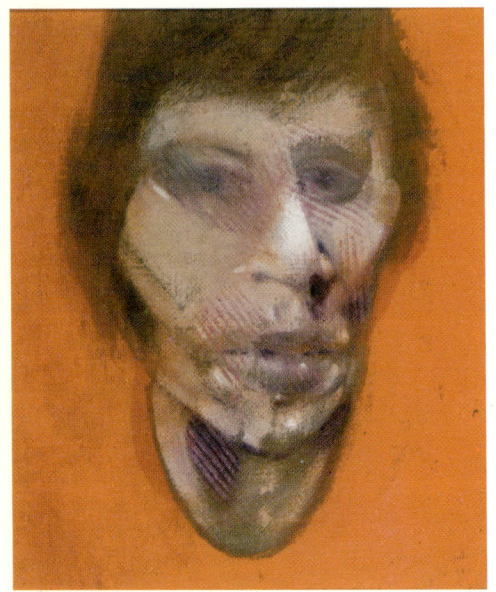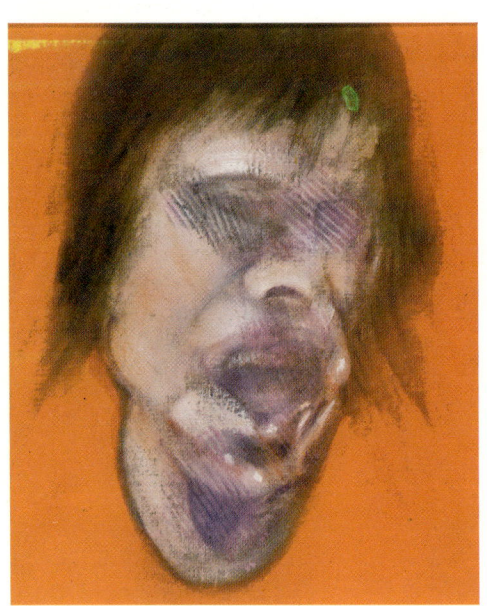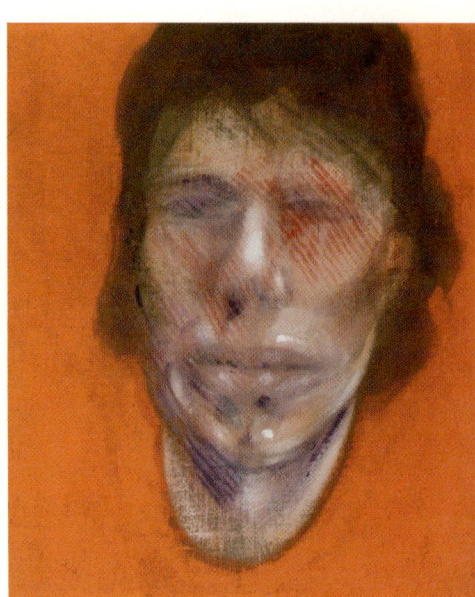

Three Studies for a Portrait (Mick Jagger) 1982 (117)

Study for Self Portrait 1981 (112)

Study of the Human Body 1982 (113)

Study from the Human Body – Figure in Movement 1982 (118)

Study for Self Portrait 1982 (116)

Diptych 1982–4 (124)

Study from the Human Body 1982–4

Study of the Human Body – from a Drawing by Ingres 1982

A Piece of Waste Land 1982 (115)

Sand Dune 1983 (122)

Triptych 1983 (123)

Oedipus and the Sphinx after Ingres 1983 (120)

Study from the Human Body 1983 (119)

Statue and Figures in a Street 1983 (121)

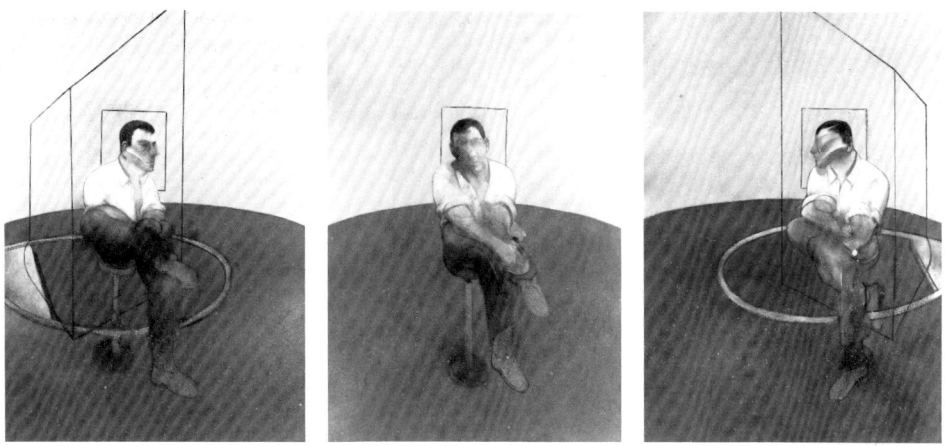

Three Studies for a Portrait of John Edwards 1984 (125)

NOTE ON TECHNIQUE
LIST OF WORKS
SELECT BIBLIOGRAPHY

Andrew Durham

NOTE ON TECHNIQUE

For Francis Bacon the aim of his art is the creation of a new and memorable image. This image is realized through 'the transforming effect of cultivated accidents of paint'. These are Bacon's own words and they provide a key insight into his painting technique: that series of physical acts by which the images in his mind, in 'a kind of pool of consciousness', become manifest in a plastic image.

The word 'cultivated' does not, he emphasizes, imply a gentle nurturing, an almost passive looking on, as the elements of the picture develop independently of the artist. Far from it. The act of painting is of fundamental importance in Bacon's work; the artist's creative and critical faculties are totally engaged at every stage in the gestation of that memorable image. Michel Leiris has remarked: 'his work carries the signs of his actions rather as a person's flesh bears the scars of an accident or an attack.'[1] And Bacon has often alluded to 'the mysterious struggle with chance'. His repeated references to 'chance' and 'accident' demonstrate his own unwillingness to analyse precisely the act of painting. He deflates the traditional, academic reverence for the craft of the painter: 'I think that painting today is pure intuition and luck and taking advantage of what happens when you splash the stuff down'[2] – yet the fact that he sees this act as a mystery is in itself important and suggests a reverential approach to his medium.

Bacon can by no means be called a conventional artist; he can no more be called a conventional painter. Nevertheless his range of materials is extremely limited in comparison with those of other artists and he restricts himself rigorously to the act of painting. Lucian Freud remarked to Lawrence Gowing that he thought Bacon's 'urgency' in painting had to do with the fact that paint was his only means of expression.[3] He does not create in any other medium: the importance to him of photography, for example, seems to have been the subsequent liberation of the painter to exploit the properties of paint without regard to narration or description, rather than his own involvement in any photographic procedures.

Since 1944 when the *Three Studies for Figures at the Base of a Crucifixion* (1) was painted, Bacon has worked exclusively on stretched canvas. The *Three Studies* themselves were painted on Sundeala board, a light and absorbent wood-fibre board, then commonly used by artists; Roy de Maistre and Graham Sutherland, both close friends of Bacon, were using Sundeala as a support at that time, de Maistre as late as 1955. But this use was dictated by economic expediency rather than considered choice. Although Sundeala had its advantages (in Bacon's opinion 'it held pastel well'), he changed to using canvas as soon as he could afford to. Initially, with *Painting 1946* (5) and *Figure in a Landscape* (2), he used the canvas in the usual way, with the commercially prepared priming as the surface on which to paint. It was not an ideal surface, however. Pastel did not adhere well, as is now all too evident in the condition of *Painting 1946*, where the pigments are flaking from the canvas and the painting is too delicate to leave the Museum of Modern Art in New York. (This is due partly to the poor adhesion between pigment and ground but

also to the nature of the pigment, mainly in the areas of cobalt violet and to the pastel-fixative which was applied to the surface and has subsequently lifted away.) More importantly for Bacon, the primed canvas did not have sufficient 'tooth' to receive the pastel or the paint in the way he wanted.

It was by accident, having run out of canvas, and painting on the back of an already used canvas in 1947–8, that he discovered the absorbent, unprimed surface which has since become his standard support. He says 'this suited the South of France' where he was working at that time. (He wants his technique 'as raw as possible' and presumably the rawness of unprimed canvas suited his way of working, of dragging the paint across the weave.) Having found a surface sympathetic to his aims and to the effect it has upon the image, he was content to look no further and he has used ready-primed canvases stretched back to front from the same artists' colourman for the last twenty or thirty years. It is interesting to note that Sutherland, who was with him in the South of France during those years, has also used canvas in this way.

Bacon does not size the canvas before beginning the picture, nor does he make a preparatory drawing; he 'draws with the brush'.

In talking of his work, Bacon draws a sharp distinction between the central image and the rest of the canvas, the background. This distinction is reflected in the materials he uses. For the background he uses acrylic paints; they can be applied quickly and smoothly but are 'not subtle enough' for the central image. He also uses emulsion house paints which, like artists' acrylics, are fast-drying and convenient for the large expanses of flat colour which provide the setting for the image. This is not to say, however, that the background is completed and the image then superimposed upon it. The background, while 'only a back to the image', is nevertheless a crucial and integral part of the whole and in terms of sequence it is modified and developed as the painting as a whole progresses. As one would imagine, Bacon is not tied to any restrictive code and there are always exceptions to his general practice. *Triptych August 1972*, for example, has the flat areas of black painted in oil greatly reduced with turpentine, and in many of the orange backgrounds he can only achieve the coloration he wants using pastel.

For the painting of the image Bacon uses predominantly, but not exclusively, artists' oil colour. He does not add extra oil or any other medium such as varnish. He does add a diluent – usually turpentine. The nature of the applied paint varies from thick dollops squeezed directly on to the canvas from the tube, high impasto and dry scumbles where the medium seems to have been soaked out, to very thin washes where a good deal of turpentine has been added to modify the tube paint. He seems to delight in the subtlety and malleability of this medium.

Picasso is the only artist whose technique Bacon will admit influenced him in any way. Again it was the 'rawness' of the technique which attracted him. Like Picasso, he will alter the properties of the paint still further, to achieve the effect he wants. He adds sand to it while wet, as in the centre panel of

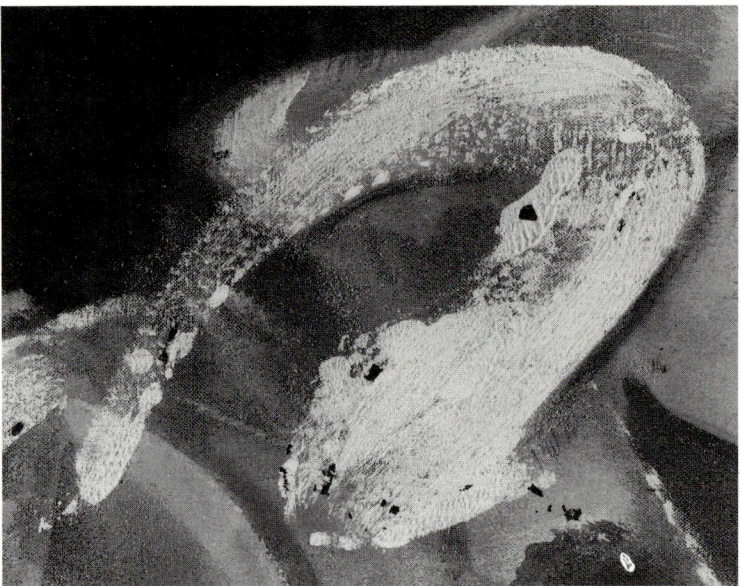

Triptych August 1972 (detail of central panel)

Triptych August 1972 where it is used to enhance the jagged impasto of the sweeping white brushstroke and also to modify the subtle modelling of the back. He leaves cotton wool and canvas fibres jutting out of the paint, as in *Reclining Woman* (37); and even, in the case of *Figure in a Landscape* (2), rubs his fingers along a dusty surface in the studio and then into the wet paint.

Bacon adapts and enhances the image with highlights of pastel and achieves amorphous, cloud-like effects, as in *Study from the Human Body*, 1983, by spraying aerosol car paints over the image.

The least painterly material he uses, and the closest he comes to the unpainterly medium of collage, is Letraset, yet it is applied in his customary, chance way and not with the precision of the graphic artist.

He does not varnish the paintings when finished nor does he use intermediary layers of varnish during painting; for areas of 'sunk' paint, for instance. The contrast between matt and gloss areas is a major aspect of the image, but Bacon again maintains that this is a result of chance. One feels, nevertheless, that over the years he has developed a profound understanding of his materials and their inherent characteristics.

The raw materials of Bacon's art are fairly straightforward. The essence of his technique is the way in which he applies them. He has said: 'I know nothing about technique'; and that it would be a waste of time for him to talk about it. This may be true of the 'painting-manual' methods of traditional painting, but for him it is his everyday practices which constitute painting technique. As Michel Leiris said, the artist asserts his presence 'not in his search for a style, but in his own particular way of doing applied to a concrete theme, in his way of placing a series of brushstrokes' and 'the paroxysm has to be introduced at least by the treatment as if the act of painting came inevitably from a sort of exacerbation, whether inherent or not in the subject matter.'[4]

Most of his painting is done with a brush: he always begins with the central image, the frenetic brushstrokes contrasting with the more sedately executed background areas, which are added and adapted as the image as a whole progresses. He may not always work fast and furiously, but the paintings he regards as the more successful are in general the ones he painted quickly.

With the brush Bacon achieves an extraordinary variety of effects. These range from the calligraphic arabesques in the background and the sharp stabbing strokes of the grass in *Figure in a Landscape* and the almost watercolourist's delicacy of the treatment of the hair in the right-hand figure of *Triptych August 1972*, to voluptuous impasto with a heavily laden brush, and the dragging of dry paint across the surface to leave encrustations rather than brushstrokes. Elsewhere he

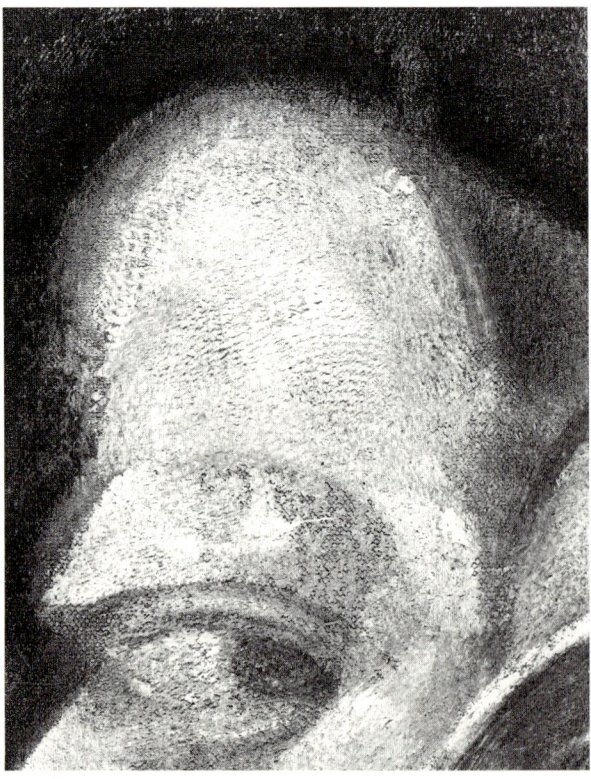

Portrait of Isabel Rawsthorne (detail), 1966

picks the brush off the surface to leave sharp peaks and serrated ridges of paint.

Bacon also manipulates the paint with his fingers, exploiting its malleable plasticity or smearing and smudging thin washes. In *Study for Portrait on Folding Bed*, 1963, blobs of paint have been squashed with the thumb. He uses a rag or a sponge to push and distort outlines and surfaces, the result being a controlled accident, or imposes an almost disciplined 'cross-hatching' by pressing a piece of corduroy against the face in a portrait. In the *Portrait of Isabel Rawsthorne*, 1966, we can see how the weave of a rag has left a lattice-work impression, which he has later enhanced by pushing pastel into the indentations when the paint has dried, and how, lower to the right, the red pastel has been dragged gently over the impasto of her collar, leaving a caked residue on the peaks of dried paint. He sometimes scrubs the canvas so the

fibres of the threads are broken and jutting, then sprays them with an aerosol, or flicks or spatters paint onto the canvas, leaving it to run and drip. He may throw or rub sand into the paint or start by throwing the paint at the canvas in the hope that the image will create itself.

It is clear that within the context of his working practices, the selective critical process whereby he adapts the accidents of his creative acts cannot be separated from the acts themselves either sequentially or emotively. To take the *Triptych Inspired by the Oresteia of Aeschylus* as an example: the jet of gore shooting from the bat-like figure is impulsively squeezed from the tube and dragged over the canvas. The rich carmine does not end in a string of paint, however, but in a brushstroke which is both controlled and considered. Chance is exploited but the result is far from arbitrary: 'the creative and the critical become a single act.'

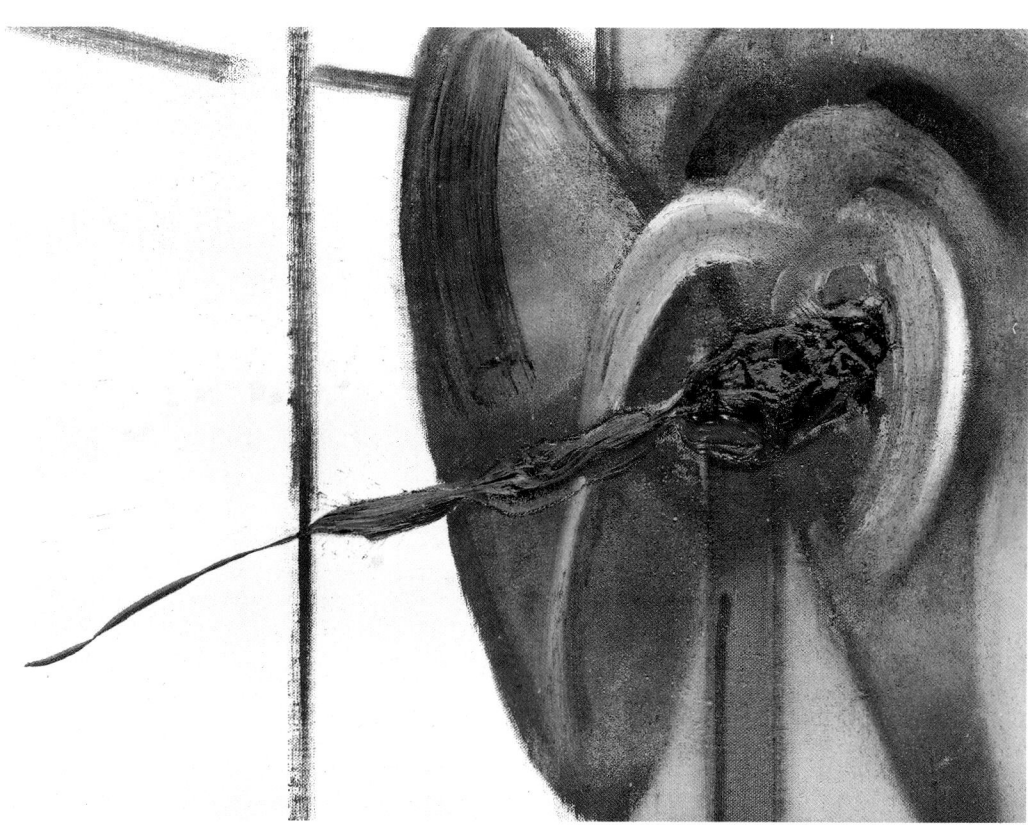

Triptych Inspired by the Oresteia of Aeschylus (detail of left-hand panel), 1981

NOTES

Unless otherwise acknowledged, all quotations are taken from conversations with the author on 1 February and 3 August 1984.

1 'Ce que m'ont dit les peintures de Francis Bacon', *Derrière le miroir*, Paris, 162 (Nov. 1966). English transl. in 'What Francis Bacon's Paintings Say to Me', *Francis Bacon: Recent Paintings*, exh. cat., London, Mar.–Apr. 1967.

2 Matthew Smith, 'A Painter's Tribute', *Matthew Smith: Paintings from 1909 to 1952*, exh. cat., London, 1953.

3 *Lucian Freud*, London and New York, 1982.

4 As Note 1, above.

LIST OF WORKS

An asterisk denotes a work loaned to the London showing only. Certain works, indicated in this list, do not appear in the exhibition but are illustrated in the plate section. Dimensions are given in centimetres and inches, height before width.

1
Three Studies for Figures at the Base of a Crucifixion 1944
Oil and pastel on hardboard, triptych, each panel 97 × 74
(37 × 29)
Tate Gallery

2
Figure in a Landscape 1945
Oil on canvas, 145 × 128 (57 × 50½)
Tate Gallery

3*
Figure Study I 1945–6
Oil on canvas, 123 × 105.5 (48½ × 41½)
Private Collection

4
Figure Study II 1945–6
Oil on canvas, 145 × 129 (57¼ × 50¾)
Kirklees Metropolitan Council

5
Painting 1946 *(Not in exhibition)*
Oil and tempera on canvas, 198 × 132 (78 × 52)
Museum of Modern Art, New York

6
Head I 1948
Oil and tempera, 103 × 75 (40½ × 29½)
Richard S. Zeisler Collection, New York

7
Head II 1949
Oil on canvas, 80.5 × 65 (31¾ × 25⅝)
Ulster Museum, Belfast

8*
Head III 1949
Oil on canvas, 81 × 66 (32 × 26)
Private Collection

9
Head VI 1949
Oil on canvas, 93 × 77 (36¾ × 30¼)
Arts Council of Great Britain

10*
Study from the Human Body 1949
Oil on canvas, 147 × 134 (57⅞ × 51½)
National Gallery of Victoria, Melbourne

11
Study for Portrait 1949 (Man in a Blue Box)
Oil on canvas, 147.5 × 131 (58 × 51½)
Museum of Contemporary Art, Chicago, Gift of Joseph and Jory Shapiro

12
Pope I 1951
Oil on canvas, 198 × 137 (78 × 54)
Aberdeen Art Gallery and Museums

13
Pope II 1951
Oil on canvas, 198 × 137 (78 × 54)
Städtische Kunsthalle Mannheim, Loan from the State of Baden-Württemberg

14
Study for Crouching Nude 1952
Oil on canvas, 198 × 137 (78 × 54)
Detroit Institute of Arts, Gift of Dr Wilhelm R. Valentiner

15
Study of a Figure in a Landscape 1952
Oil on canvas, 198 × 137 (78 × 54)
Phillips Collection, Washington

16*
Study after Velasquez's Portrait of Pope Innocent X 1953
Oil on canvas, 153 × 118 (60¼ × 46½)
Des Moines Art Center, Coffin Fine Arts Trust Fund, 1980

17
Study for a Portrait 1953
Oil on canvas, 152.5 × 118 (60 × 46½)
Kunsthalle, Hamburg

18
Man with Dog 1953
Oil on canvas, 152 × 117 (59⅞ × 46)
Albright-Knox Art Gallery, Buffalo, New York, Gift of Seymour H. Knox, 1955

19*
Sphinx I 1953
Oil on canvas, 199.5 × 137 (78½ × 54)
Private Collection

20
Study of a Baboon 1953
Oil on canvas, 198 × 137 (78 × 54)
Museum of Modern Art, New York, James Thrall Soby Bequest

21
Three Studies of the Human Head 1953
Oil on canvas, triptych, each panel 61 × 51 (24 × 20)
Private Collection

22
Two Figures 1953 *(Not in exhibition)*
Oil on canvas, 152.5 × 116.5 (60 × 45⅞)
Private Collection

23
Study for a Portrait 1953
Oil on canvas, 198 × 137 (78 × 54)
Private Collection, Switzerland

24*
Two Figures in the Grass 1954

Oil on canvas, 152 × 117 ($59\frac{3}{4} × 46\frac{1}{8}$)
Private Collection

25*
Figure with Meat 1954
Oil on canvas, 129 × 122 ($50\frac{7}{8} × 48$)
Art Institute of Chicago, Harriott A. Fox Fund

26*
Pope 1954
Oil on canvas, 152.5 × 116.5 ($60 × 45\frac{7}{8}$)
Private Collection, Switzerland

27
Study for Portrait II (after the Life Mask of William Blake)
1955
Oil on canvas, 61 × 51 ($24 × 20$)
Tate Gallery

28
Study for Portrait III (after the Life Mask of William
Blake) 1955
Oil on canvas, 60 × 51 ($24 × 20$)
Capricorn Art International SA, Panama

29
Chimpanzee 1955
Oil on canvas, 152.5 × 117 ($60 × 46$)
Staatsgalerie Stuttgart

30
Figures in a Landscape 1956–7
Oil on canvas, 152.5 × 118 ($60 × 46\frac{1}{2}$)
Birmingham Museums and Art Gallery

31
Study for Figure IV 1956–7
Oil on canvas, 152.5 × 116 ($59\frac{7}{8} × 45\frac{5}{8}$)
*Art Gallery of South Australia, Adelaide, Gift of the
Contemporary Art Society, London, 1959*

32*
Study for Portrait of Van Gogh II 1957
Oil on canvas, 198 × 142 ($78 × 56$)
Edwin Janss, Thousand Oaks, California

33
Study for Portrait of Van Gogh VI 1957
Oil on canvas, 202.5 × 142 ($79\frac{3}{4} × 56$)
Arts Council of Great Britain

34
Figure in Landscape (Miss Diana Watson) 1957
Oil on canvas, 198 × 137 ($78 × 54$)
Private Collection, London

35
Miss Muriel Belcher 1959
Oil on canvas, 74 × 67.5 ($29 × 26\frac{1}{2}$)
Private Collection

36
Head of Woman 1960
Oil on canvas, 84 × 67.5 ($33 × 26\frac{1}{2}$)
Private Collection

37
Reclining Woman 1961
Oil on canvas, 198.5 × 141.5 ($78\frac{1}{4} × 55\frac{3}{4}$)
Tate Gallery

38*
Study from Innocent X 1962
Oil on canvas, 198 × 145 ($78 × 57\frac{1}{8}$)
Mr M. Riklis

39*
Three Studies for a Crucifixion 1962
Oil on canvas, triptych, each panel 198 × 145 ($78 × 57$)
Solomon R. Guggenheim Museum, New York

40*
Lying Figure with Hypodermic Syringe 1963
Oil on canvas, 198 × 145 ($78 × 57$)
Private Collection, Switzerland

41
Landscape near Malabata, Tangier 1963
Oil on canvas, 198 × 145 ($78 × 57$)
Private Collection

42*
Three Figures in a Room 1964
Oil on canvas, triptych, each panel 198 × 147 ($78 × 57\frac{7}{8}$)
*Musée National d'Art Moderne, Centre Georges
Pompidou, Paris*

43*
Study for Portrait (Isabel Rawsthorne) 1964
Oil on canvas, 198 × 147.5 ($78 × 58$)
Private Collection

44
Three Studies for Head of Isabel Rawsthorne 1965
Oil on canvas, triptych, each panel 35.5 × 30.5 ($14 × 12$)
*Robert and Lisa Sainsbury Collection, University of East
Anglia, Norwich*

45*
Crucifixion 1965
Oil on canvas, triptych, each panel 197.2 × 147 ($77\frac{5}{8} × 57\frac{7}{8}$)
*Staatsgalerie Moderner Kunst, Munich, Gift of the Galerie-
Vereins, Munich eV*

46
After Muybridge – Study of the Human Figure in Motion
– Woman Emptying a Bowl of Water, and Paralytic Child
on All Fours 1965
Oil on canvas, 198 × 147.5 ($78 × 58$)
Stedelijk Museum, Amsterdam

47*
Three Studies for Portrait of Lucian Freud 1965
Oil on canvas, triptych, each panel 35.5 × 30.5 ($14 × 12$)
Private Collection

48
Study of Isabel Rawsthorne 1966
Oil on canvas, 35.5 × 30.5 ($14 × 12$)
Louise and Michel Leiris Collection

49*
Portrait of George Dyer Staring at a Blind-cord 1966
Oil on canvas, 198 × 147.5 ($78 × 58$)
Private Collection

50*
Three Studies of Muriel Belcher 1966
Oil on canvas, triptych, each panel 35.5 × 30.5 ($14 × 12$)
Private Collection

51
Portrait of George Dyer Riding a Bicycle 1966
Oil on canvas, 198 × 147.5 (78 × 58)
Private Collection, New York

52
Portrait of Isabel Rawsthorne Standing in a Street in Soho
1967
Oil on canvas, 198 × 147.5 (78 × 58)
*Staatliche Museen Preussischer Kulturbesitz, Nationalgalerie,
Berlin*

53
Triptych Inspired by T.S. Eliot's Poem 'Sweeney
Agonistes' 1967
Oil on canvas, each panel 198 × 147.5 (78 × 58)
*Hirshhorn Museum and Sculpture Garden, Smithsonian
Institution, Washington DC*

54
Three Studies of Isabel Rawsthorne 1967
Oil on canvas, 119 × 152.5 (46⅞ × 60)
*Staatliche Museen Preussischer Kulturbesitz, Nationalgalerie,
Berlin*

55
Portrait of George Dyer in a Mirror 1967–8 *(Not in
exhibition)*
Oil on canvas, 198 × 147.5 (78 × 58)
Thyssen-Bornemisza Collection, Lugano, Switzerland

56
Two Studies of George Dyer with Dog 1968 *(Not in
exhibition)*
Oil on canvas, 198 × 147.5 (78 × 58)
Private Collection

57
Two Studies for a Portrait of George Dyer 1968
Oil on canvas, 198 × 147.5 (78 × 58)
*Sara Hildén Foundation, Sara Hildén Art Museum, Tampere,
Finland*

58
Triptych – Two Figures Lying on a Bed with Attendants
1968 *(Not in exhibition)*
Oil on canvas, each panel 198 × 147.5 (78 × 58)
Present whereabouts unknown

59*
Three Studies of Lucian Freud 1969
(Right-hand panel only)
Oil on canvas, triptych, each panel 198 × 147.5 (78 × 58)
Private Collection

60*
Study for Bullfight No.1 1969
Oil on canvas, 198 × 147.5 (78 × 58)
Private Collection

61
Lying Figure 1969 *(Not in exhibition)*
Oil on canvas, 198 × 147.5 (78 × 58)
Private Collection

62
Second Version of Study for Bullfight No.1 1969
Oil on canvas, 198 × 147.5 (78 × 58)
Private Collection, New York

63
Three Studies of Henrietta Moraes 1969
Oil on canvas, triptych, each panel 35.5 × 30.5 (14 × 12)
Capricorn Art International SA, Panama

64
Three Studies for Portraits Including Self Portrait 1969
Oil on canvas, triptych, each panel 35.5 × 30.5 (14 × 12)
Private Collection

65
Study of Nude with Figure in a Mirror 1969
Oil on canvas, 198 × 147.5 (78 × 58)
Private Collection

66
Self Portrait 1969
Oil on canvas, 35.5 × 30.5 (14 × 12)
Private Collection

67
Study of Henrietta Moraes 1969
Oil on canvas, 35.5 × 30.5 (14 × 12)
Private Collection, South Africa

68
Study for Portrait 1970 *(Not in exhibition)*
Oil on canvas, 198 × 147.5 (78 × 58)
Private Collection, France

69*
Triptych – Studies from the Human Body 1970
Oil on canvas, each panel 198 × 147.5 (78 × 58)
Jacques Hachuel

70
Studies of George Dyer and Isabel Rawsthorne 1970
Oil on canvas, diptych, each panel 35.5 × 30.5 (14 × 12)
Private Collection

71
Three Studies of the Male Back 1970
Oil on canvas, triptych, each panel 198 × 147.5 (78 × 58)
Kunsthaus Zürich, Vereinigung Zürcher Kunstfreunde

72*
Self Portrait 1970
Oil on canvas, 152 × 147.5 (59⅞ × 58)
Private Collection

73
Triptych – Studies of the Human Body 1970
Oil on canvas, each panel 198 × 147.5 (78 × 58)
Marlborough International Fine Art

74
Second Version of 'Painting 1946' 1971
Oil on canvas, 198 × 147.5 (78 × 58)
Museum Ludwig, Cologne

75
Self Portrait 1971
Oil on canvas, 35.5 × 30.5 (14 × 12)
Louise and Michel Leiris Collection

76*
Study for Portrait of Lucian Freud (Sideways) August 1971
Oil on canvas, 198 × 147.5 (78 × 58)
Private Collection, London

77
Triptych 1971
Oil on canvas, each panel 198 × 147.5 (78 × 58)
Private Collection, USA

78
Three Studies of Figures on Beds 1972
Oil and pastel on canvas, triptych, each panel 198 × 147.5
(78 × 58)
Private Collection

79
Self Portrait 1972
Oil on canvas, 35.5 × 30.5 (14 × 12)
Gilbert de Botton, Switzerland

80
Three Studies for Self Portrait 1972
Oil on canvas, triptych, each panel 35.5 × 30.5 (14 × 12)
Private Collection

81
Triptych August 1972
Oil on canvas, each panel 198 × 147.5 (78 × 58)
Tate Gallery

82
Three Portraits: Posthumous Portrait of George Dyer,
Self Portrait, Portrait of Lucian Freud 1973
Oil on canvas, triptych, each panel 198 × 147.5 (78 × 58)
Private Collection

83*
Study for Self Portrait 1973
Oil on canvas, 35.5 × 30.5 (14 × 12)
Private Collection

84
Self Portrait 1973
Oil on canvas, 198 × 147.5 (78 × 58)
Halvor N. Astrup

85*
Triptych May–June 1973
Oil on canvas, each panel 198 × 147.5 (78 × 58)
Mr and Mrs Saul P. Steinberg

86*
Self Portrait 1973
Oil on canvas, 198 × 147.5 (78 × 58)
Private Collection

87*
Triptych March 1974
Oil on canvas, each panel 198 × 147.5 (78 × 58)
Private Collection, Madrid

88
Sleeping Figure 1974
Oil on canvas, 198 × 147.5 (78 × 58)
A. Carter Pottash

89
Seated Figure 1974
Oil and pastel on canvas, 198 × 147.5 (78 × 58)
Gilbert de Botton, Switzerland

90
Study for a Human Body (Man Turning on the Light)
1973–4

Oil and acrylic on canvas, 198 × 147.5 (78 × 58)
Royal College of Art, London

91*
Three Studies for a Portrait of Peter Beard 1975
Oil on canvas, triptych, each panel 35.5 × 30.5 (14 × 12)
Private Collection

92
Three Studies for a Portrait (Peter Beard) 1975
Oil on canvas, triptych, each panel 35.5 × 30.5 (14 × 12)
Private Collection

93*
Portrait of a Dwarf 1975
Oil on canvas, 158.5 × 58.5 (62½ × 23)
Private Collection, Sydney, Australia

94
Three Figures and a Portrait 1975
Oil and pastel on canvas, 198 × 147.5 (78 × 58)
Tate Gallery

95
Studies from the Human Body 1975
Oil on canvas, 198 × 147.5 (78 × 58)
Gilbert de Botton, Switzerland

96*
Figure in Movement 1976
Oil on canvas, 198 × 147.5 (78 × 58)
Private Collection

97
Portrait of Michel Leiris 1976
Oil on canvas, 35.5 × 30.5 (14 × 12)
Louise and Michel Leiris Collection

98*
Triptych 1976
Oil and pastel on canvas, each panel 198 × 147.5 (78 × 58)
Private Collection, France

99*
Figure Writing Reflected in a Mirror 1976
Oil on canvas, 198 × 147.5 (78 × 58)
Private Collection

100
Three Studies for Self Portrait 1976
Oil on canvas, triptych, each panel 35.5 × 30.5 (14 × 12)
Thyssen-Bornemisza Collection, Lugano, Switzerland

101
Triptych 1974–7
(Centre panel revised 1977)
Oil and pastel on canvas, each panel 198 × 147.5 (78 × 58)
The Artist

102
Study for Portrait (Michel Leiris) 1978
Oil on canvas, 35.5 × 30.5 (14 × 12)
Louise and Michel Leiris Collection

103*
Landscape 1978
Oil and pastel on canvas, 198 × 147.5 (78 × 58)
Private Collection

104*
Painting 1978
Oil on canvas, 198 × 147.5 (78 × 58)
Private Collection, Monaco

105
Figure in Movement 1978
Oil and pastel on canvas, 198 × 147.5 (78 × 58)
Private Collection, Los Angeles

106
Jet of Water 1979
Oil on canvas, 198 × 147.5 (78 × 58)
Private Collection, Switzerland

107*
Triptych – Studies of the Human Body 1979
Oil on canvas, each panel 198 × 147.5 (78 × 58)
Private Collection

108
Sphinx – Portrait of Muriel Belcher 1979
Oil on canvas, 198 × 147.5 (78 × 58)
National Museum of Modern Art, Tokyo

109*
Three Studies for Self Portrait 1979
Oil on canvas, triptych, each panel 37.5 × 31.8 (14¾ × 12½)
Private Collection

110
Triptych Inspired by the Oresteia of Aeschylus 1981
Oil on canvas, each panel 198 × 147.5 (78 × 58)
Marlborough International Fine Art

111*
Sand Dune 1981
Oil and pastel on canvas, 198 × 147.5 (78 × 58)
Private Collection

112
Study for Self Portrait 1981
Oil on canvas, 198 × 147.5 (78 × 58)
Von der Heydt-Museum, Wuppertal

113*
Study of the Human Body 1982
Oil and pastel on canvas, 198 × 147.5 (78 × 58)
Musée National d'Art Moderne, Centre Georges Pompidou, Paris

114
Water from a Running Tap 1982
Oil on canvas, 198 × 147.5 (78 × 58)
Private Collection

115
A Piece of Waste Land 1982
Oil on canvas, 198 × 147.5 (78 × 58)
The Artist

116*
Study for Self Portrait 1982
Oil on canvas, 198 × 147.5 (78 × 58)
Private Collection, New York

117
Three Studies for a Portrait (Mick Jagger) 1982
Oil and pastel on canvas, triptych, each panel 35.5 × 30.5
(14 × 12)
Paul Jacques Schupf

118
Study from the Human Body – Figure in Movement 1982
Oil on canvas, 198 × 147.5 (78 × 58)
Marlborough International Fine Art

119
Study from the Human Body 1983
Oil and pastel on canvas, 198 × 147.5 (78 × 58)
Menil Foundation Collection, Houston

120
Oedipus and the Sphinx after Ingres 1983
Oil on canvas, 198 × 147.5 (78 × 58)
Private Collection, California

121
Statue and Figures in a Street 1983
Oil and pastel on canvas, 198 × 147.5 (78 × 58)
The Artist

122
Sand Dune 1983
Oil and pastel on canvas, 198 × 147.5 (78 × 58)
Ernst Beyeler, Basle

123
Triptych 1983
Oil and pastel on canvas, each panel 198 × 147.5 (78 × 58)
Marlborough International Fine Art

124
Diptych 1982–4
Study from the Human Body 1982–4
Study of the Human Body – from a Drawing by Ingres
1982
Oil and pastel on canvas, each panel 198 × 147.5 (78 × 58)
The Artist

125
Three Studies for a Portrait of John Edwards 1984
Oil on canvas, triptych, each panel 198 × 147.5 (78 × 58)
The Artist

SELECT BIBLIOGRAPHY

Compiled by Krzysztof Cieszkowski

The bibliography is divided into seven sections: **1**, Writings by and interviews with Bacon; **2**, Books; **3**, Sections of books; **4**, Articles and reviews; **5**, Films; **6**, One-man exhibition catalogues; **7**, Group exhibition catalogues.

Sections 1 and 4–7 are arranged chronologically; sections 2 and 3 are arranged in alphabetical order by author (section 3 by the author of the section on Bacon rather than the editor of the book, if different).

Although sections 6 and 7 list exhibition catalogues rather than exhibitions *per se*, they also record exhibitions for which no catalogue was published, or where no catalogue has been located. Section 6

includes catalogues of exhibitions in which Bacon exhibited on his own, or those which are concerned exclusively with his works. In section 7, entries specify the number of works by Bacon included in the exhibition.

Square brackets indicate information supplied from sources other than the item itself.

This bibliography represents a selection from a full bibliography, which has more detailed, as well as additional entries. For further details of this, please contact the compiler at the Tate Gallery.

1. Writings by and Interviews with Bacon

'Francis Bacon: Matthew Smith – A Painter's Tribute', in: London, Tate Gallery, exh. cat., *Matthew Smith: Paintings from 1909 to 1952*, [Sept.–Oct.] 1953, p. 12.

[Statement] in: New York, Museum of Modern Art, exh. cat., *The New Decade: 22 European Painters and Sculptors*, May–Aug. 1955, pp. 60–4.

'"Der Tradition eine neue Wendung geben": ein Gespräch mit dem Maler Francis Bacon, von Stephen Spender', in: *Die Weltwoche*, 19 Oct. 1962, p. 27.

'Francis Bacon Talking to David Sylvester' [recorded 21 Oct. 1962, broadcast on BBC Third Programme 23 Mar. 1963]; publ. as 'The Art of the Impossible', *Sunday Times* colour supplement, 14 July 1963, pp. 13–18; reprinted in London, Marlborough Fine Art, exh. cat., July–Aug. 1963, pp. 3–5, and in Sylvester (interview 1) 1975, pp. 8–29.

'From a Conversation with Francis Bacon' [interview with Michael Peppiatt, Aug., Dec. 1963], *Cambridge Opinion*, 37, [Jan.] 1964, pp. 48–9.

'Sunday night Francis Bacon' [filmed May 1966, transmitted on BBC television 18 Sept. 1966, written and dir. by Michael Gill; publ. as *From Interviews with Francis Bacon by David Sylvester* in London, Marlborough New London Gallery, exh. cat., Mar.–Apr. 1967, pp. 26–38; reprinted in Sylvester (interview 2) 1975, pp. 30–67.

'Playmen intervista: Francis Bacon, conversazione senza complessi con un grande pittore "intrattabile"' [interview with Michael Pergolani], *Playmen*, Oct. 1970, pp. 17ff.

[Interview with Gavin Millar] in *Francis Bacon, Grand Palais 1971*, BBC television film. [1971].

'Francis Bacon, ou la réalité piégée' [interview with Claude Bouyère], *Jardin des arts*, Nov. 1971, pp. 6–7.

'Est-il méchant?' [interview], *L'Express*, 15–21 Nov. 1971, pp. 98–100.

'Marguerite Duras s'entretient avec Bacon', *Quinzaine littéraire*, 16–30 Nov. 1971, pp. 16–17.

'Entretien avec Francis Bacon' [interview with G. Lascault], *L'Art vivant*, Dec. 1971.

[Broadcast on BBC Radio 3] publ. as 'Tearing the Human Image to Bits – Andrew Forge, Francis Bacon and Michael Levey Talk about Titian', *Listener*, 6 Mar. 1972, pp. 334–5.

'Francis Bacon' [interview with Jacques Saraben, 25 Mar. 1972], *Instants*, Bordeaux, no. 2 (1972), pp. 2–3.

'Vivo in una fogna dorata: intervistato a Londra il pittore che ha preso il posto di Picasso' [interview with Franco de Giorgi], *Gente*, 5 Sept. 1974, pp. 28–31.

'Lucian Freud, Francis Bacon: Turner at the Academy' [letter to the Editor], *The Times*, 26 Sept. 1974, p. 15.

'The Exhilarated Despair of Francis Bacon' [extracts from interviews with David Sylvester publ. in Sylvester 1975], *Art News*, May 1975, pp. 26–31.

'Francis Bacon: Remarks from an Interview with Peter Beard, Edited by Henry Geldzahler', in: New York, Metropolitan Museum of Art, exh. cat., Mar.–July 1975, pp. 14–20; extracts publ. in French tr. in *Galerie-jardin des arts*, Apr. 1975, pp. 72–4.

David Sylvester: Interviews with Francis Bacon, London: Thames and Hudson; New York: Pantheon Books, 1975. Contents: interview 1 (Oct. 1962, originally publ. 23 Mar. 1963); interview 2 (May 1966, originally publ. Mar. 1967); interview 3 (privately recorded in three sessions, Dec. 1971, July 1973, Oct. 1973); interview 4 (privately recorded in two sessions, Sept. 1974). French, Spanish and Swedish editions, publ. 1976–7, contain interviews 1–4 [as above], and interview 5 (recorded 23 Apr. 1975 by London Weekend Television, transmitted 29/30 Nov. 1975 in *Aquarius* as 'Sunday Night Francis Bacon', and incorporating material from privately recorded session).

[Texts repr. in] ed. Andrew Brighton and Lynda Morris, *Towards Another Picture: An Anthology of Writings by Artists Working in Britain 1945–1977*, Nottingham: Midland Group, 1977, pp. 100–2, 121, 166–7.

'I Only Paint for Myself' [interview with Edward Behr], *Newsweek*, 24 Jan. 1977, pp. 46–9.

'Madeleine Chapsal: Francis Bacon et la joie' [interview], *L'Express*, 7–13 Feb. 1977, pp. 10–13.

[Interview with Michel Lancelet and Edward Behr] in *Fenêtre sur . . . Peintres de notre temps: Francis Bacon*, film by French Television (Antenne 2), dir. Georges Paumier, transmitted 19 Apr. 1977.

'Ernesto Gonzalez: "El optimismo es una forma de imbecilidad": entrevista con Francis Bacon', *Cuadernos para el Dialogo*, 8 Apr. 1978, pp. 51–3.

David Sylvester: Interviews with Francis Bacon,

1962–1979, new and enlarged edition, London: Thames and Hudson, 1980. Contents: interviews 1–5 (as in 1975 ed.); interview 5 (as in French, Spanish and Swedish eds, 1976–7); interviews 6–7 (privately recorded in three sessions, Mar., Aug., Sept. 1979).

'An Interview with Francis Bacon' [interview with David Sylvester] [repr. from Sylvester 1980]. *The Times Literary Supplement*, 21 Nov. 1980, p. 1318.

'Bringing Home Bacon' [interview with Miriam Gross]. *Observer*, 30 Nov. 1980; republ. in Italian tr. as 'Confessione di un genio disperato: a colloquio col grande pittore Francis Bacon', in *Gente* [1981], pp. 174, 179, 182–4.

'I Think about Death Every Day' [interview with Joshua Gilder], *Saturday Review*, New York, Sept. 1981, pp. 36–9; repr. in *Flash Art*, 112, May 1983, pp. 17–21.

'Francis Bacon and David Sylvester: An Unpublished Interview' [Mar. 1982], in: Paris, Galerie Maeght-Lelong, exh. cat., Jan.–Feb. 1984 (*Repères: cahiers d'art contemporain*, no. 10), pp. 21, 29–32.

'Francis Bacon: "Je prends la réalité en sténo"' [interview with Maiten Bouisset], *Le Matin*, 19 Jan. 1984, pp. 27–8.

[Interview with Pierre Daix, recorded 19 Jan. 1984] in *Après Hiroshima . . . Francis Bacon*, film for French television (A2), presented by Pierre Daix, dir. Pierre-André Boutang and P. Collin, in series 'Désirs des arts'; screened on A2, 5 Feb. 1984.

Francis Bacon dans et autour de la peinture: 'Je voudrais casser les styles' [incl. interview with Jacques Michel], *Le Monde*, 26 Jan. 1984, pp. 12–13.

'Entretien: Francis Bacon' [interview with Alice Bellony-Rewald], *Beaux-Arts Magazine*, 10, Feb. 1984, pp. 28–33.

'Falstaff 1984: un entretien avec Francis Bacon' [interview with France Huser], *Le Nouvel Observateur*, 3 Feb. 1984.

2. Books

Alley, Ronald, and John Rothenstein. *Francis Bacon* (introd. by John Rothenstein, text by Ronald Alley). London: Thames and Hudson; New York: Viking Press, 1964.

Calhoun, Alice Ann. 'Suspended Projections: Religious Roles and Adaptable Myths in John Hawkes's Novels, Francis Bacon's Paintings, and

Ingmar Bergman's Films' (PhD thesis, Department of English, University of South Carolina, 1979). Ann Arbor (Mich.): University Microfilms International, copyright 1979.

Davies, Hugh Marlais. *Francis Bacon: The Early and Middle Years, 1928–1958* (PhD dissertation, Princeton University, Department of Art and Archaeology, Aug. 1975). New York, London: Garland Publishing, 1978.

Deleuze, Gilles. *Francis Bacon: Logique de la Sensation.* [Paris]: Editions de la Différence ('La Vue le texte'), 1981.

Duckers, Alexander. *Francis Bacon: 'Painting 1946'.* Stuttgart: Philipp Reclam jun. ('Werk-monographien zur bildenden Kunst in Reclams Universal-Bibliothek', Nr. 145), 1971.

Leiris, Michel. *Francis Bacon, ou la vérité criante.* [Paris]: Fata Morgana/Scholies, 1974.

Leiris, Michel. *Francis Bacon, face et profil.* Paris: Albin Michel; Munich: Prestel-Verlag; Milan: Rizzoli; Barcelona: Ediciones Poligrafa, 1983; tr. John Weightman, *Francis Bacon, Full Face and in Profile.* Oxford: Phaidon; New York: Rizzoli, 1983.

Rothenstein, Sir John. *Francis Bacon.* Milan: Fratelli Fabbri Editori, 1963; London: Purnell ('The Masters', 71); Paris: Hachette, 1967.

Russell, John. *Francis Bacon.* London: Methuen ('Art in Progress'), 1964.

Russell, John. *Francis Bacon.* London: Thames and Hudson, 1971; Paris: Les Editions du Chêne; Berlin: Prophylaen Verlag; rev. ed.: London: Thames and Hudson; New York: Oxford University Press ('World of Art'), 1979.

Schreiner, Richard Gus. 'The Concrete Imagination: A Perspective on Selected Works of Francis Bacon and Edvard Munch' (EdD dissertation, Teachers College, Columbia University, 1980). Ann Arbor (Mass.): University Microfilms International, copyright 1980.

Sylvester, David. *Interviews with Francis Bacon.* London: Thames and Hudson; New York: Pantheon Books, 1975. *Samtal med Francis Bacon.* [Stockholm]: Forum, [1976]. *Francis Bacon: l'art de l'impossible – entretiens avec David Sylvester.* Preface by Michel Leiris, Geneva: Editions Albert Skira ('Les sentiers de la création'), 1976. *Entrevistas con Francis Bacon.* Barcelona: Ediciones Poligrafa, 1977; rev. ed. *Interviews with Francis Bacon, 1962–1979.* London: Thames and Hudson, 1980. *Gespräche mit Francis Bacon.* Munich: Prestel-Verlag, 1982.

Trucchi, Lorenza. *Francis Bacon.* Milan: Fratelli Fabbri Editori ('Le grandi monografie: pittori d'oggi'), 1975. Tr. John Shepley; New York: Harry N. Abrams, 1975; London: Thames and Hudson, 1976.

Waldegg, Joachim Heusinger von. *Francis Bacon: Schreiender Papst, 1951.* Mannheim: Städtische Kunsthalle ('Kunst und Dokumentation'), [1980].

3. Sections of Books

Berger, John. 'The Worst Is Not Yet Come', in: ed. Paul Barker: *Arts in Society.* London: Fontana/Collins, 1977. pp. 66–73; previously publ. as 'The Worst Is Not Yet', in *New Society,* London, 6 Jan. 1972; rev. version publ. as 'Francis Bacon and Walt Disney', in Berger: *About Looking.* London: Writers and Readers, 1980, pp. 111–18.

Brighton, Andrew, and Lynda Morris (eds). *Towards Another Picture: An Anthology of Writings by Artists Working in Britain 1945–1977.* Nottingham: Midland Group, 1977, pp. 100–2, 121, 166–7.

Flores, Felix Gabriel. 'El desesperante mundo de Francis Bacon', in: Flores: *Cronicas Europeas.* Cordoba (Argentina): Universidad Nacional de Cordoba, 1972, pp. 244–51.

Ironside, Robin. *Painting Since 1939.* London: Longmans Green, for The British Council, 1947, pl. between pp. 24 and 25.

Kramer, Hilton. 'The Problem of Francis Bacon', *The Age of the Avant-garde: An Art Chronicle of 1956–1972.* London: Secker and Warburg, 1974, pp. 374–7 (originally publ. in *New York Times,* 17 Nov. 1968).

Read, Herbert. *Art Now: An Introduction to the Theory of Modern Painting and Sculpture.* London: Faber and Faber, 1933, pl. 101.

Read, Herbert. *Contemporary British Art.* Harmondsworth (Middx): Penguin Books, 1957; rev. ed. 1964; pp. 33–5, pl. IV.

Rothenstein, John. *Brave Day, Hideous Night: Autobiography 1939–1965 (1).* London: Hamish Hamilton, 1966, pp. 105–6, 219.

Rothenstein, Sir John. *Modern English Painters, III: Wood to Hockney.* London: Macdonald, 1974, pp. 157–75, 242–3.

Rothenstein, John. *Time's Thievish Progress: Autobiography III.* London: Cassell, 1970, pp. 12, 79–80, 82–94, 238.

Russell, John. [Section] in Bryan Robertson, John Russell and Lord Snowdon: *Private View.* London, Edinburgh: Nelson, 1965, pp. 62–7.

Soby, James Thrall. *Contemporary Painters.* New York: Museum of Modern Art, 1948, pp. 145–6, 151.

4. Articles and Reviews

'The 1930 Look in British Decoration', *Studio,* Aug. 1930, pp. 140–1 (illus.).

P.G. Konody. 'Art and Artists: The Mayor Gallery', *Observer,* 23 Apr. 1933, p. 14.

'Mr Francis Bacon', *The Times,* 16 Feb. 1934, p. 9.

Michael Ayrton. 'Art', *Spectator,* 13 Apr. 1945, p. 335.

Raymond Mortimer. 'At the Lefevre', *New Statesman,* 14 Apr. 1945, p. 239.

Roger Marvell. 'New Pictures', *New Statesman,* 16 Feb. 1946, p. 119.

'Lefevre Gallery: New English Paintings', *The Times,* 19 Feb. 1946, p. 6.

Patrick Heron. 'Letter from London', *Magazine of Art,* Nov. 1948, pp. 273, 277.

Wyndham Lewis. 'Round the London Art Galleries', *Listener,* 12 May 1949, pp. 811–12 (illus.).

Wyndham Lewis. 'Round the London Art Galleries', *Listener,* 17 Nov. 1949, p. 860 (illus.).

Pierre Rouve. 'Francis Bacon and Robin Ironside', *Art News and Review,* 19 Nov. 1949, p. 3.

Nevile Wallis. 'Nightmare', *Observer,* 20 Nov. 1949, p. 6.

'Survivors', *Time,* 21 Nov. 1949, p. 44.

'Art Exhibitions: Mr. Francis Bacon', *The Times,* 22 Nov. 1949, p. 7.

Robert Melville. 'Francis Bacon', *Horizon,* Dec. 1949–Jan. 1950, pp. 419–23 (illus.).

Patrick Heron. 'Francis Bacon', *New Statesman,* 3 Dec. 1949, pp. 643–4.

Cora J. Gordon. 'London Commentary', *Studio,* Feb. 1950, pp. 61–3.

Wyndham Lewis. 'Round the London Art Galleries', *Listener,* 21 Sept. 1950, p. 368.

'Hanover Gallery: Mr. Francis Bacon's Paintings', *The Times,* 22 Sept. 1950, p. 6.

W. Matvyn Wright. 'Francis Bacon and Hilly', *Art News and Review,* 23 Sept. 1950, p. 4.

Nevile Wallis. 'Francis Bacon', *Observer,* 24 Sept. 1950, p. 6.

Robin Ironside. 'England's Poets in Paint', *Art News,* Oct. 1950, pp. 20–3, 67 (illus.).

Robert Melville. 'The Iconoclasm of Francis Bacon', *World Review,* Jan. 1951, pp. 63–4 (illus.).

Nevile Wallis. 'Francis Bacon', *Observer,* 23 Dec. 1951, p. 6 (illus.).

Michael Middleton. 'Work in Progress', *Art News and Review,* 29 Dec. 1951, p. 4.

Eric Newton. 'Francis Bacon', *Time and Tide,* 29 Dec. 1951, pp. 1279–80.

Sam Hunter. 'Francis Bacon: The Anatomy of Horror', *Magazine of Art,* Jan. 1952, pp. 11–15.

David Sylvester. 'The Paintings of Francis Bacon', *Listener,* 3 Jan. 1952, pp. 28–9 (illus.).

John Berger. 'Francis Bacon', *New Statesman,* 5 Jan. 1952, pp. 11–12.

'Hanover Gallery: Mr. Bacon's Paintings', *The Times,* 7 Jan. 1952, p. 8.

'Points of View: Bacon and Balthus', *Art News and Review,* 26 Jan. 1952, p. 7.

'Perspex'. 'Shafts from Apollo's Bow: The Return of the Problem Picture', *Apollo,* Feb. 1952, p. 33.

Robert Melville. 'A Note on the Recent Paintings of

Francis Bacon', *World Review,* Feb. 1952, pp. 31–2 (illus.).

Michael Greenwood. 'Ape and Bacon', *Granta,* Cambridge, 8 Mar. 1952, pp. 20–1.

Nevile Wallis. 'Vertebrate', *Observer,* 14 Dec. 1952, p. 11.

John Russell. 'Reality Plus', *Sunday Times,* 14 Dec. 1952.

'Mr. Bacon's New Paintings: African Animals', *The Times,* 16 Dec. 1952, p. 11.

David Sylvester. 'Round the London Art Galleries', *Listener,* 18 Dec. 1952, p. 1040.

David Waring. 'Hanover Gallery', *Art News and Review,* 27 Dec. 1952, p. 5.

David Sylvester. 'Realism Old and New', *Britain To-day,* Jan. 1953, pp. 10–13.

Vernis. 'Master of the Monstrous', *Connoisseur,* Mar. 1953, p. 34.

Sam Hunter. 'Francis Bacon: "An Acute Sense of Impasse"', *Art Digest,* 15 Oct. 1953, p. 16 (illus.).

'Snapshots from Hell', *Time,* 19 Oct. 1953, pp. 62–3 (illus.).

Dorothy Gees Seckler. 'Francis Bacon', *Art News,* Nov. 1953, pp. 42–3.

'Social and Anti-social', *Time and Tide,* [Nov. 1953].

James Thrall Soby. 'Mr. Francis Bacon', *Saturday Review,* New York, 7 Nov. 1953, pp. 48–9 (illus.); repr. in Soby: *Modern Art and the New Past,* 1957, pp. 126–30.

'Mr. Francis Bacon's New Paintings: Extraordinary Use of Photographs', *The Times,* 13 Nov. 1953, p. 10.

M.H. Middleton. 'Old Surrealism and New Realism', *Spectator,* 20 Nov. 1953, pp. 568, 570.

Pierre Rouve. 'Two Worlds', *Art News and Review,* 28 Nov. 1953, p. 8.

James Fitzsimmons. 'Paintings of Apes and Madmen at Durlacher Brothers', *Arts and Architecture,* Los Angeles, Jan. 1954, p. 30 (illus.).

David Sylvester. 'Francis Bacon', *Britain To-day,* Feb. 1954, pp. 23–6 (illus.).

Herbert Read. 'Le due tendenze inglesi: Ben Nicholson, Francis Bacon e Lucian Freud al padiglione della Gran Bretagna', *La Biennale di Venezia,* Apr.–June 1954, pp. 53–7 (illus.).

Nevile Wallis. 'Trio', *Observer,* 13 June 1954, p. 11.

'Apparitions of Evil: Mr. Francis Bacon's New Paintings', *The Times,* 14 June 1954, p. 5.

Eric Newton. 'Three Contemporary Artists', *Time and Tide,* 19 June 1954, p. 817.

Bernard Boles. 'Mostly Bacon', *Arts News and Review,* 26 June 1954, p. 4.

John Berger. 'Round the Galleries', *New Statesman,* 26 June 1954, p. 830.

Eleanor C. Munro. 'Bacon, Hepworth, Scott', *Art News,* Oct. 1954, pp. 51–2.

Hilton Kramer. 'British Trio', *Arts Digest,* 15 Oct. 1954, p. 22.

'The Paintings of Mr. Bacon: A Prophet of Doom', *The Times,* 24 Jan. 1955, p. 3.

David Sylvester. 'Round the London Galleries', *Listener,* 27 Jan. 1955, p. 162.

Stephen Bone. 'Horrors and Abstractions', *Time and Tide,* 29 Jan. 1955, pp. 134–5.

Lawrence Alloway. 'Notes on Francis Bacon', *Art News and Review,* 5 Feb. 1955, p. 4.

Lawrence Alloway. 'Art News from London', *Art News,* Mar. 1955, pp. 17, 59–60.

Robert Melville. 'Exhibitions', *Architectural Review,* Apr. 1955, pp. 270–1 (illus.).

James Thrall Soby. 'Reg Butler and Francis Bacon', *Saturday Review,* New York, 7 May 1955, pp. 60–2 (illus.).

Alan Clutton-Brock. 'Round the London Galleries', *Listener,* 7 July 1955, p. 7.

Robert Melville. 'Exhibitions', *Architectural Review,* Sept. 1955, pp. 189–90 (illus.).

'Francis Bacon', *Current Bibliography Yearbook,* New York: H.W. Wilson Co., 1957, pp. 33–5 (illus.).

John Russell. 'Across the Channel', *Sunday Times,* 24 Feb. 1957.

Nevile Wallis. 'Bacon and Sironi', *Observer,* 24 Mar. 1957, p. 13 (illus.).

John Russell. 'A Private Mythology', *Sunday Times,* 24 Mar. 1957.

'Mr. Francis Bacon's Virtuosity: Van Gogh Translated', *The Times,* 26 Mar. 1957, p. 3.

Alan Clutton-Brock. 'Round the London Art

Galleries', *Listener*, 28 Mar. 1957, p. 522.

James Burr. 'The Baconian Van Gogh: Hanover Gallery', *Art News and Review*, 30 Mar. 1957, p. 6.

Eric Newton. 'Francis Bacon', *Time and Tide*, 30 Mar. 1957, pp. 385–6.

David Sylvester. 'In Camera', *Encounter*, Apr. 1957, pp. 22–4 (illus.).

Jean-Albert Cartier. 'Une imagerie "bourée de souvenirs": Francis Bacon', *Jardin des arts*, Apr. 1957, pp. 346–7 (illus.).

Basil Taylor. 'Bacon v. Van Gogh', *Spectator*, 5 Apr. 1957, p. 443.

John Golding. 'Lust for Death', *New Statesman*, 6 Apr. 1957, p. 438.

Denys Sutton. 'Francis Bacon', *Financial Times*, 16 Apr. 1957; repr. in Sutton: *Delights of a Dilettante*, Westwood Press, 1980, pp. 214–16.

Lawrence Alloway. 'Art News from London: Style and Bacon', *Art News*, May 1957, pp. 48, 58 (illus.).

'Portrait Gallery: Francis Bacon', *Sunday Times*, 5 May 1957, p. 3 (illus.).

G.S. Whittet. 'London Commentary', *Studio*, June 1957, pp. 187–90.

M.H. Middleton. 'Art', *Spectator*, 25 June 1957, p. 778.

Patrick Heron. 'London', *Arts*, Sept. 1957, pp. 12–13 (illus.).

Luce Hoctin. 'Francis Bacon et la hantise de l'homme', *XXe siècle*, Christmas 1958, pp. 53–5 (illus.).

'Francis Bacon's Paintings', *The Times*, 17 June 1959, p. 7.

Keith Sutton. 'Man at the Centre', *Art News and Review*, 20 June 1959, pp. 1, 8 (illus.).

Eric Newton. 'Imagination and Fantasy', *Time and Tide*, 20 June 1959, p. 708.

Alan Clutton-Brock. 'Round the London Art galleries', *Listener*, 25 June 1959, p. 1118.

Lawrence Alloway. 'Francis Bacon', *Art International*, 1960 [vol. 4 nos. 2–3], pp. 62–3 (illus.).

Eric Newton. 'Paintings of Visual Nausea', *Guardian*, 24 Mar. 1960.

Stephen Spender. 'As Bacon Sees Us', *Observer*, 27 Mar. 1960, p. 24 (illus.).

'Mr. Bacon's Comment on Humanity', *The Times*, 28 Mar. 1960, p. 6.

David Carritt. 'Bacon – The Art of Success', *Evening Standard*, 29 Mar. 1960 (illus.).

Denys Sutton. 'Francis Bacon', *Financial Times*, 29 Mar. 1960, p. 15.

Terence Mullaly. 'Bacon Looks at Man: The Veneer's Stripped Away', *Daily Telegraph*, 30 Mar. 1960 (illus.).

Alan Clutton-Brock. 'Round the London Art Galleries', *Listener*, 31 Mar. 1960, p. 582 (illus.).

Horace Shipp. 'Current Shows and Comments: The Dark Is Light Enough – Francis Bacon at the Marlborough', *Apollo*, Apr. 1960, p. 92.

Eric Newton. 'Recent paintings by Francis Bacon', *Time and Tide*, 2 Apr. 1960, p. 376.

Basil Taylor. 'Bacon's Progress, Epstein's Past', *Sunday Times*, 3 Apr. 1960.

R.B. Kitaj. 'Bacon in the Nut House Again', *London American*, 7–13 Apr. 1960, p. 14.

Lawrence Alloway. 'Dr. No's Bacon', *Art News and Review*, 9 Apr. 1960, pp. 4–5 (illus.).

Alan Bowness. 'London', *Arts*, May 1960, pp. 20–1 (illus.).

Michael Strauss. 'Current and Forthcoming Exhibitions: London', *Burlington Magazine*, May 1960, pp. 221, 223–4 (illus.).

John Russell. 'Art News from London: Francis Bacon', *Art News*, Summer 1960, p. 52, 68.

Robert Melville. 'Exhibitions: Paintings and Sculpture', *Architectural Review*, June 1960, pp. 422–4 (illus.).

G.S. Whittet. 'London Commentary', *Studio*, July 1960, p. 29 (illus.).

Jules Langsner. 'Art News from Los Angeles: Bacon, Bloom, Los Angeles Group', *Art News*, Dec. 1960, p. 46.

N.E.B. 'Artist Bacon Explores New Fields', *Manchester Guardian*, 17 Feb. 1961.

Terence Mullaly. 'Sincerity of Francis Bacon: Rewarding Show at Nottingham', *Daily Telegraph*, 20 Feb. 1961 (illus.).

Anthony Tucker. 'Beyond Despair', *Guardian*, 23 Feb. 1961.

Stephen Spender. 'Francis Bacon at Nottingham', *Listener*, 23 Feb. 1961, p. 360 (illus.).

Helen Lessore. 'A Note on the Development of Francis Bacon's Painting', *X, A Quarterly Review*, Mar. 1961, pp. 23–6 (illus.).

Howard Griffin. 'Francis Bacon: "Case-history Painting"', *Studio*, May 1961, pp. 164–9 (illus.).

Stephen Spender. 'Francis Bacon', *Quadrum*, XI, ([Dec.] 1961), pp. 47–58 (illus.).

'"Ich habe nichts gegen Päpste": Francis Bacon, Ausstellung in der Kunsthalle von Mannheim', *Aktuell*, Munich, 1962 (no. 31), pp. 34–6 (illus.).

'Bacon: Angst in Öl', *Der Spiegel*, Hamburg, 1962 (no. 26), pp. 59–61 (illus.).

Terence Mullaly. 'Bacon's Works Shock Viewer: Painter with Eye to the Realities', *Daily Telegraph*, 24 May 1962 (illus.).

Eric Newton. 'Mortal Conflict', *Manchester Guardian*, 24 May 1962, p. 7 (illus.).

'The Horrific Vision of Mr. Francis Bacon', *The Times*, 24 May 1962, p. 7 (illus.).

David Carritt. 'Bacon: The Painter Who Can Evoke the Horror', *Evening Standard*, 25 May 1962, p. 18 (illus.).

John M. Nash. 'The Private Obsessions of Francis Bacon', *Yorkshire Post*, 25 May 1962 (illus.).

'The Observer Profile: Francis Bacon', *Observer Weekly Review*, 27 May 1962, p. 23 (illus.).

Nigel Gosling. 'Report from the Underworld', *Observer Weekly Review*, 27 May 1962, p. 27 (illus.).

W.G. Archer. 'Dramas in Paint', *Sunday Telegraph*, 27 May 1962 (illus.).

John Russell. 'Titian Crossed with Tussaud', *Sunday Times*, 27 May 1962 (illus.).

Denys Sutton. 'Francis Bacon – Too Shrill a Cry?', *Financial Times*, 29 May 1962, p. 22 (illus.).

'The Horrific Theme in Visual Art', *The Times*, 29 May 1962, p. 15.

Keith Roberts. 'Mr. Francis Bacon in the Woodshed', *Time and Tide*, 31 May 1962, pp. 19–20 (illus.).

Jasia Reichardt. 'Les Expositions à l'étranger: Londres', *Aujourd'hui*, June 1962, p. 50 (illus.).

Jasia Reichardt. 'Developments in Style V: Francis Bacon', *The London Magazine*, June 1962, pp. 38–44 (illus.).

Edward Lucie-Smith. 'Images of Our Time', *Listener*, 7 June 1962, p. 998 (illus.).

Hugh Graham. 'Francis Bacon', *The Spectator*, 8 June 1962, pp. 753–4.

'Distort into Reality', *Time*, 8 June 1962, p. 60 (illus.).

Julian Exner. 'Orpheus und Hamm: zwei bedeutende Londoner Ausstellungen, Barbara Hepworth und Francis Bacon', *Frankfurter Rundschau*, 13 June 1962 (illus.).

Hilde Spiel. 'Zwei englische Maler: zu Ausstellungen Graham Sutherlands und Francis Bacons', *National Zeitung*, Basel, 17 June 1962.

Hermann Dannecker. 'Die Schrecken des Francis Bacon', *Schwäbische Donau Zeitung*, 18 June 1962.

David Sylvester. 'Francis Bacon', *New Statesman*, 22 June 1962, pp. 915–16.

Edwin Mullins. 'Academy Myths and Private Images', *Apollo*, July 1962, pp. 406–10 (illus.).

Anita Brookner. 'Current and Forthcoming Exhibitions: London', *Burlington Magazine*, July 1962, pp. 313–17 (illus.).

Egon A. Joos. 'Zwischen Konzentrationslager und Atombombe', *Allgemeine Zeitung*, Mannheim, 19 July 1962.

Bernard Smith. 'Image and Meaning in Recent Painting', *Listener*, 19 July 1962, pp. 93–4.

Margarethe Krieger. 'Über die menschliche Angst', *Mannheimer Morgen*, 20 July 1962, p. 22 (illus.).

Richard Biedrzynski. 'Anatomie des Schreckens', *Stuttgarter Zeitung-Postausgabe*, 20 July 1962.

H. Morgenthaler. 'Der Mensch in Bacons Schreckenskammer', *Badische Neueste Nachrichten*, Karlsruhe, 21 July 1962 (illus.).

David Sylvester. 'Der sensationelle Maler', *Deutsche Zeitung mit Wirtschaftszeitung*, Cologne and Stuttgart, 25 July 1962 (illus.).

Doris Schmidt. 'Bilder aus der Schreckenskammer', *Süddeutsche Zeitung*, 25 July 1962, p. 12 (illus.).

Hanns Theodor Flemming. 'Zwischen Alptraum und Faszination', *Die Welt*, 25 July 1962, supplement p. 7 (illus.).

Robert Melville. 'Exhibitions: Painting and Sculpture', *Architectural Review*, Aug. 1962, pp. 132–4 (illus.).

G.S. Whittet. 'London Commentary: You Can't Write Off the British', *Studio*, Aug. 1962, pp. 72–3 (illus.).

G.S. Whittet. 'G.S. Whittet Says . . .', *Studio*, Aug. 1962, p. 43.

Gert Kalow. 'Nachrichten vom Tod', *Frankfurter Allgemeine Zeitung*, 1 Aug. 1962, supplement p. 20 (illus.).

A.G. 'Furcht und Mitleid', *Wormser Zeitung*, 3 Aug. 1962.

Will Grohmann. 'Akt, Tier, Papst oder van Gogh', *Die Zeit*, 3 Aug. 1962, supplement p. 8 (illus.).

Wolfram Siebeck. 'Gesichter schreien hinter Glaswänden', *Der Mittag*, Düsseldorf, 4 Aug. 1962 (illus.).

John Anthony Thwaites. 'Das Gemeinste was es je gegeben hat', *Deutsche Zeitung mit Wirtschaftszeitung*, Cologne and Stuttgart, 6 Aug. 1962, p. 10.

Eo Plunien. 'Viel Gruselei für die Magengrube: das Kruditäten-Kabinett des Mr. Francis Bacon', *Abendpost*, Frankfurt, 7 Aug. 1962 (illus.).

Kurt Neufert. 'Das Phänomen Francis Bacon', *Donau-Kurier*, Ingoldstadt, 7 Aug. 1962.

Ulrich Seelmann-Eggbert. 'In der Zwangsjacke des Abwegigen', *Rheinische Post*, Düsseldorf, 7 Aug. 1962.

Egbert Hoehl. 'Im Zeitaler der Angst', *Die andere Zeitung*, Hamburg, 9 Aug. 1962 (illus.).

Hanno Reuther. 'Stumm im Käfig des Terrors', *Frankfurter Rundschau*, 11 Aug. 1962, p. 42 (illus.).

H.H. 'Zwischen KZ und Atombombe', *Vorwärts*, Bonn, 15 Aug. 1962.

Hermann Dannecker. 'Im Schreckenskabinett des Francis Bacon', *Weser-Kurier*, Bremen, 17 Aug. 1962.

Armin Mohler. 'Europa im Aschenregen: der Goya unserer Zeit, Francis Bacon', *Christ und Welt*, Stuttgart, 24 Aug. 1962.

Wilhelm Westecker. 'Der deformierte Mensch Francis Bacons', *Der Tagesspiegel*, 25 Aug. 1962 (illus.).

Gertrude de Alencar. 'Francis Bacon "der Andere"', *Basler Nachrichten*, 26 Aug. 1962, p. 11 (illus.).

Michael Fried. 'Francis Bacon's Achievement', *Arts Magazine*, Sept. 1962, pp. 28–9 (illus.).

'Gli spietati racconti di Bacon', *Successo*, Milan, Sept. 1962.

Luigi Carluccio. 'Un mondo di paure e di ceneri', *Gazzetta del Popolo*, Turin, 11 Sept. 1962 (illus.).

Marziano Bernardi. 'Il massimo pittore inglese vivente da una disperata immagine dell'uomo', *La Stampa*, 11 Sept. 1962.

Angelo Dragone. 'Ossessione e orrida angoscia dietro i mostri di Francis Bacon', *Stampe Sera*, Turin, 11 Sept. 1962 (illus.).

Salvator Bruno. 'Espone a Torino Francis Bacon, uno dei maggiori pittori inglesi', *L'Unità*, 11 Sept. 1962.

Filippo Scroppo. 'I personaggi del pittore Bacon', *L'Unità*, 11 Sept. 1962 (illus.).

Marco Valsecchi. 'Dipinge l'abdicazione dell'uomo', *Il Giorno*, Milan, 15 Sept. 1962 (illus.).

Mario de Micheli. 'Un allucinata testimonianza del nostro tempo', *L'Unità*, 22 Sept. 1962 (illus.).

Elvira Salvi. 'L'urlo e il terrore nelle tele di Bacon: la mostra di Torino – un risalto impressionante et attuale', *Il Giornale di Brescia*, 28 Sept. 1962 (illus.).

'Torino: una mostra di Francis Bacon', *Emporium*, Bergamo, Oct. 1962, pp. 174–5 (illus.).

Giorgio Mascherpa. 'Un fitto mistero circonda la vita di Bacon', *Gente*, Milan, 5 Oct. 1962, pp. 69–70.

Carla Lonzi. 'Mostra di Francis Bacon a Torino', *L'Approdo* (Florence), 8 Oct. 1962.

Giovanni Urbani. 'La pittura di Bacon', *Il Punto*, Rome, 13 Oct. 1962, p. 27 (illus.).

Renzo Biasion. 'Francis Bacon dipinge gli orrori della guerra', *L'Oggi*, Milan, 18 Oct. 1962.

Stephen Spender. '"Der Tradition eine neue Wendung geben": ein Gespräch mit dem Maler Francis Bacon', *Die Weltwoche*, 19 Oct. 1962, p. 27 (illus.).

Raffaele Carrieri. 'Francis Bacon cavalca una tigre', *Epoca*, Milan, 21 Oct. 1962 (illus.).

Luciano Budigna. 'Dipingendo si ispira a fotografie

non riuscite', *La Settimana*, Rome, 21 Oct. 1962.

Norbert Lynton. 'London letter: Bacon, Davie, Kokoschka', *Art International*, 25 Oct. 1962, pp. 68–70 (illus.).

Marco Valsecchi. 'Bacon', *Il Giorno*, Milan, 25 Oct. 1962.

Marisa Volpi. 'A Francis Bacon piace la letteratura', *Avanti!*, 28 Oct. 1962 (illus.).

L.B. 'Mostre d'arte: Francis Bacon', *Corriere della Sera*, 28 Oct. 1962.

Richard Hasli. 'Francis Bacon: Ausstellung im Kunsthaus Zürich', *Neue Zürcher Zeitung*, 31 Oct. 1962, supplement p. 9 (illus.).

Antonio del Guercio. 'Bacon e il pittore della disumanizzazione dell'eta contemporanea', *Italia Moderna*, Milan, Nov. 1962 (illus.).

U.H. '"Der Mensch als des Menschen Feind"', *Zürchsee Zeitung*, 3 Nov. 1962 (illus.).

John Ashbery. 'Bacon in Zurich, the "School of Paris" at the Charpentier', *New York Herald Tribune*, European ed., Paris, 7 Nov. 1962, p. 6 (illus.).

Domenico Cara. 'Francis Bacon e le sue figure ex-umane', *Vie Nuove*, Rome, 15 Nov. 1962, pp. 51–3 (illus.).

Fritz Billeter. 'Francis Bacon', *National-Zeitung*, Basel, 22 Nov. 1962.

E.M.L. 'Malerei mit dem Zerrspiegel', *Deutsche Tagespost*, Würzburg, 28 Nov. 1962.

Lucia Moholy. 'Current and Forthcoming Exhibitions', *Burlington Magazine*, Dec. 1962, p. 567.

Ronald Alley. 'Francis Bacon', *Cimaise*, Jan.–Feb. 1963, pp. 12–25.

Magda van Emde Boas. 'Wider die Trägheit des Herzens', *Die Welt*, 1 Feb. 1963.

Eric Newton. 'Power', *Guardian*, 12 July 1963, p. 9 (illus.).

'New Work by Henry Moore and Francis Bacon', *The Times*, 12 July 1963, p. 5 (illus.).

Nigel Gosling. 'Vision and Nightmare', *Observer Weekend Review*, 14 July 1963, p. 27 (illus.).

'The Art of the Impossible', [interview with David Sylvester], *Sunday Times Colour Magazine*, 14 July 1963, pp. 13–18 (illus.).

John Richardson. 'The Private Hells of Francis Bacon . . .', *Evening Standard*, 17 July 1963, p. 8 (illus.).

Terence Mullaly. 'Age Mirrored in Bacon's Art: Distortion Used to Shock Viewer', *Daily Telegraph*, 19 July 1963.

Edwin Mullins. 'Another Look at Bacon', *Sunday Telegraph*, 21 July 1963 (illus.).

John Russell. 'On Bacon's Own Terms', *Sunday Times*, 21 July 1963.

Denys Sutton. 'The Paradoxes of Francis Bacon', *Financial Times*, 23 July 1963, p. 20 (illus.).

Bryan Robertson. 'Moore and Bacon', *Listener*, 25 July 1963, pp. 127–8 (illus.).

Andrew Forge. 'What Art Can Encompass', *New Statesman*, 26 July 1963, p. 120.

Bettina Wadia. 'Henry Moore and Francis Bacon', *Arts Review*, 27 July–10 Aug. 1963, pp. 2, 19 (illus.).

Keith Roberts. 'Current and Forthcoming Exhibitions: Francis Bacon and Henry Moore', *Burlington Magazine*, Aug. 1963, pp. 381–2.

Alastair Gordon. 'Art in the Modern Manner', *Connoisseur*, Aug. 1963, p. 270.

Peter Gorsen. 'Die Revision des Porträts durch Francis Bacon', *Das Kunstwerk*, Aug.–Sept. 1963, pp. 4, 18–21, 33 (illus.).

Lawrence Gowing. 'Another Look at Francis Bacon', *Observer Weekend Review*, 11 Aug. 1963, p. 18 (illus.).

[Denys Sutton]. 'Editorial: Knights of the Razor', *Apollo*, Sept. 1963, pp. 170–1 (illus.).

Mark Roskill. 'Francis Bacon as a Mannerist', *Art International*, 25 Sept. 1963, pp. 44–8 (illus.).

Robin Denny. 'A Note on Henry Moore and Francis Bacon', *Art International*, 25 Sept. 1963, pp. 49–52 (illus.).

John Russell. 'Peer of the Macabre: Francis Bacon', *Art in America*, Oct. 1963, pp. 100–3 (illus.).

Andrew Forge. 'Bacon: The Paint of Screams', *Art News*, Oct. 1963, pp. 38–41, 55–6 (illus.).

Gene Baro. 'Bond Street and Battersea', *Arts Magazine*, Oct. 1963, pp. 32–4.

Emily Genauer. 'The Art of Francis Bacon: Utterly Defeated Flesh', *New York Herald Tribune*, 17 Oct. 1963.

L.E. Levick. 'Figures Do the Twist in Bacon's Realism', *New York Journal American*, 19 Oct. 1963.

Brian O'Doherty. 'On the Strange Case of Francis Bacon', *New York Times*, 20 Oct. 1963 (illus.).

David Sylvester. 'Enter Bacon, with the Bacon Scream', *New York Times Magazine*, 20 Oct. 1963, pp. 24–5, 57–9, 62, 64 (illus.).

'"Man the Accident"', *Newsweek*, 21 Oct. 1963, pp. 60–1 (illus.).

Irving Sandler. 'In the Art Galleries', *New York Post*, 27 Oct. 1963 (illus.).

Lawrence Campbell. 'Francis Bacon', *Art News*, Nov. 1963, p. 13.

'In the Grand Manner', *Time*, 1 Nov. 1963, pp. 82–3 (illus.).

Lawrence Alloway. 'Francis Bacon: A Great, Shocking, Eccentric Painter', *Vogue*, New York, 1 Nov. 1963, pp. 136–9 (illus.).

Max Kozloff. 'Francis Bacon', *The Nation*, 16, 23 Nov. 1963; repr. in Kozloff: *Renderings: Critical Essays on a Century of Modern Art*. London: Studio Vista, 1970, pp. 159–63 (illus.).

Jane Harrison. 'Dissent on Francis Bacon', *Arts Magazine*, Dec. 1963, pp. 18–23 (illus.).

Alastair Gordon. 'Art in the Modern Manner', *Connoisseur*, Dec. 1963, pp. 256–7 (illus.).

Georgine Oeri. 'The Object of Art', *Quadrum*, 16, [1964], pp. 4–26 (ref. pp. 11–12) (illus.).

Dore Ashton. 'Notes on Francis Bacon', *Arts & Architecture*, Los Angeles, Jan. 1964, pp. 6–7, 32 (illus.).

Jasia Reichardt. 'Some Notes on Painting in Britain', *Cambridge Opinion*, no. 37, Jan. 1964, pp. 14–23.

Michael Peppiatt. 'From a Conversation with Francis Bacon' (interviews), *Cambridge Opinion* 37, [Jan. 1964], pp. 48–9.

Douglas Cooper. 'Blake and Bacon', *New Statesman*, 24 Jan. 1964, p. 120.

Franz Schulze. 'Bacon Excels in Mastery of Mood, Message', *Chicago News*, 1 Feb. 1964 (illus.).

Richard L. Feigen. 'Bacon Paintings Could Shock or Haunt Viewers', *Chicago Tribune*, 2 Feb. 1964 (illus.).

Lawrence Alloway. 'Bacon le convulsif, ou l'angoisse sied aux héros', *XXe siècle*, May 1964, pp. 27–34 (illus.).

David Piper. 'Painting of the Month: Francis Bacon's "Figures in a Landscape"', *Listener*, 11 June 1964, pp. 953–5 (illus.); previously broadcast on Third Network; extract publ. in *Painting of the Month* (BBC), June 1964, pp. 57–60 (illus.).

'Robert Melville Has a Look at a Book about Francis Bacon', *Studio*, July 1964, pp. 10–15 (illus.).

Keith Roberts. 'Current and Forthcoming Exhibitions: London', *Burlington Magazine*, Aug. 1964, pp. 393–4 (illus.).

John Russell. 'In the Galleries', *Art News*, Sept. 1964, p. 49.

David Thompson. 'Introduktion til nutidigt Engelsk maleri', *Louisiana-Revy*, Humelbaek, Sept. 1964, pp. 14–20 (illus.).

Philip Leider. 'Francis Bacon by John Rothenstein and Ronald Alley', *Artforum*, Jan. 1965, p. 51.

'No Pinpointing', *Times Literary Supplement*, 6 May 1965, pp. 341, 346 (illus.).

Brian O'Doherty. 'On the Strange Case of Frances [sic] Bacon', *Art Journal*, Spring 1965, pp. 288–90.

James Burr. 'Horror and Harmony', *Apollo*, July 1965, p. 63 (illus.).

John Russell. 'Francis Bacon', *Aujourd'hui*, July 1965, pp. 64–7 (illus.).

David Thompson. 'From the Sinister to the Sweet', *Observer Weekend Review*, 11 July 1965, p. 20.

John Russell. 'On Bearable Terms with the Worst', *Sunday Times*, 11 July 1965.

'Bacon and Moore again in Powerful Relation', *The Times*, 14 July 1965, p. 15.

Keith Roberts. 'Current and Forthcoming Exhibitions: London', *Burlington Magazine*, Aug. 1965, p. 441 (illus.).

John Russell. 'Art News from London', *Art News*, Sept. 1965, pp. 50–1 (illus.).

Andrew Forge. 'Painting of the Month: "Seated Figure" by Francis Bacon', *Listener*, 9 Dec. 1965, pp. 964–5 (illus.); previously broadcast on 'Study Session' (Third Programme); extract publ. in *Painting of the Month* (BBC), Dec. 1965, pp. 105–8 (illus.).

F.M. 'Bacon', *Domus*, May 1966, pp. 51–2 (illus.).

Paul Johnson. 'London Diary', *New Statesman*, 23 Sept. 1966, p. 424.

J. Kervyn de Meerendre, P.R.J. Stanton. 'Bacon's Paintings' [letters in response to Paul Johnson], *New Statesman*, 30 Sept. 1966, p. 476.

[Issue devoted to Francis Bacon], *Derrière le miroir* 162 (Nov. 1966). Contents: pp. 1–10 Michel Leiris: 'Ce que m'ont dit les peintures de Francis Bacon'; pp. 17–26 'Ce qu'a dit Francis Bacon à David Sylvester' (illus.).

'The Coroner's Report', *Time*, 18 Nov. 1966, pp. 90–1 (illus.).

R.C. Kenedy. 'Francis Bacon', *Art International*, Dec. 1966, pp. 24, 28–9 (illus.).

Robert Melville. 'The Recent Paintings of Francis Bacon', *Motif*, 13, [1967], pp. 4–16 (illus.).

Julien Alvard. 'Paris: The Grand Inquisitor', *Art News*, Jan. 1967, pp. 24–5.

Julien Alvard. 'Francis Bacon', *Aujourd'hui*, Jan. 1967, pp. 186–7 (illus.).

James Burr. 'London Galleries: Convulsions of Mind and Body', *Apollo*, Mar. 1967, p. 225 (illus.).

Nigel Gosling. 'Francis Bacon: Man Not Nude but Naked', *Observer Colour Supplement*, 5 Mar. 1967, pp. 16–24, 27–8 (illus.).

Nigel Gosling. 'Heroic Pessimism on a Bicycle', *Observer Review*, 12 Mar. 1967, p. 25.

John Russell. *Sunday Times*, 12 Mar. 1967 (illus.).

Charles Spencer. 'Bacon Becomes Detached', *New York Times*, 14 Mar. 1967.

Guy Brett. 'Francis Bacon's Imagery Less Intense', *The Times*, 15 Mar. 1967, p. 10 (illus.).

Robert Melville. 'Corkscrew Twist', *New Statesman*, 17 Mar. 1967, p. 382 (illus.).

Paul Oliver. 'Francis Bacon', *Arts Review*, 18 Mar. 1967, pp. 80–1 (illus.).

Paul Overy. 'Two Views of Atrocities', *Listener*, 30 Mar. 1967, p. 434 (illus.).

Keith Roberts. 'Current and Forthcoming Exhibitions: London', *Burlington Magazine*, Apr. 1967, pp. 256–9 (illus.).

Joseph Rykwert. 'Exhibitions in London', *Domus*, Apr. 1967, pp. [51–2] (illus.).

Robert Melville. 'Francis Bacon', *Studio*, Apr. 1967, pp. 192–5 (illus.).

Bryan Robertson. 'Figure-device', *Spectator*, 14 Apr. 1967, p. 430.

John Russell. 'London: Simultaneous Bacon', *Art News*, May 1967, p. 18 (illus.).

Robert Melville. 'The Arresting Image', *Architectural Review*, Oct. 1967, pp. 301–2 (illus.).

Henry J. Seldis. 'Brilliant Francis Bacon Display in New York', *Los Angeles Times*, [Nov. 1968], pp. 1, 19 (illus.).

Gregory Battcock. 'Francis Bacon: First Major New York Gallery Show', *Arts Magazine*, Nov. 1968, pp. 46–7 (illus.).

'Bacon in New York', *The Times*, 8 Nov. 1968, p. 10 (illus.).

Hilton Kramer. 'The Problem of Francis Bacon', *New York Times*, 17 Nov. 1968 (illus.); republ. in Kramer: *The Age of the Avant-garde: An Art Chronicle of 1956–1972*, London: Secker and Warburg, 1974, pp. 374–7.

John Russell. 'Bacon's Universal Room', *Sunday Times*, 17 Nov. 1968 (illus.).

'Prelude to Butchery', *Time*, 29 Nov. 1968, p. 42 (illus.).

Lawrence Gowing. 'Pigment Figment', *Art News*, Dec. 1968, pp. 42–5 (illus.).

'Francis Bacon: "Photography Has Completely Altered Figurative Painting"', *Creative Camera*, Dec. 1968, pp. 442–3 (illus.).

'Gallery-hopping: Francis Bacon', *Newsweek*, 2 Dec. 1968, p. 34 (illus.).

Michael Peppiatt. 'Francis Bacon's New Paintings', *Art International*, 20 Dec. 1968, pp. 35–8 (illus.).

Robert Pincus-Witten. 'New York', *Artforum*, Jan. 1969, pp. 56–7 (illus.).

Alastair Gordon. 'Art in the Modern Manner', *Connoisseur*, Jan. 1969, pp. 32–3 (illus.).

Dore Ashton. 'New York Commentary', *Studio International*, Jan. 1969, pp. 45–6 (illus.).

Pierre Descargues. 'Pourquoi donc faire faire son

portrait?', *Connaissance des arts*, Mar. 1969, cover and pp. 70–7 (illus.).

Joseph T. Butler. 'The American Way with Art: Francis Bacon – Recent Paintings', *Connoisseur*, Apr. 1969, pp. 270–1 (illus.).

R.M. Dippel. 'Van Gogh en Bacon', *Museumjournaal*, Apr. 1969, pp. 100–1 (illus.).

John Russell. 'Francis Bacon at Sixty', *Art in America*, Jan.–Feb. 1970, pp. 106–11 (illus.).

'Playmen intervista: Francis Bacon, conversazione senza complessi con un grande pittore "intrattabile"' [interview with Michael Peppiatt], *Playmen*, Oct. 1970, pp. 17ff (illus.).

John Russell. 'Francis Bacon: A Retrospective and a Preview', *Horizon*, New York, Autumn 1971, pp. 78–95 (illus.).

H.C. 'Grande première à Paris de Francis Bacon, No. 1 de l'index CDA '71', *Connaissance des arts*, Oct. 1971, p. 31 (illus.).

Maurice Eschapasse. 'Francis Bacon: un corps à corps avec l'homme seul en piste dans un espace oppressant', *Plaisir de France*, Oct. 1971, pp. 2–7 (illus.).

John Gruen. 'Francis Bacon, a Night's Journey and a Day', *Vogue*, London, Oct. 1971, pp. 86ff (illus.).

Richard Cork. 'Why Bacon Will *Paint* his Life Story', *Evening Standard*, 4 Oct. 1971, p. 19 (illus.).

R.C. 'Francis Bacon prend sa place parmi les grands', *Le Figaro*, 8 Oct. 1971, p. 30 (illus.).

Sabine Marchand. 'Une oeuvre "hors courants" qui trouve sa source dans l'Expressionnisme', *Le Figaro*, 8 Oct. 1971, p. 30 (illus.).

Pierre Schneider. 'The Savage God', *Observer*, 10 Oct. 1971.

'Le peintre anglais Bacon', *L'Amateur d'art*, 21 Oct. 1971 (illus.).

Guy Brett. 'Francis Bacon in Paris: Figures in a Room', *The Times*, 27 Oct. 1971, p. 17 (illus.).

Nigel Gosling. 'Magnificent Mr. Bacon', *Observer Review*, 31 Oct. 1971, p. 30.

Michael Shepherd. 'Bacon Abroad', *Sunday Telegraph*, 31 Oct. 1971.

Eddie Wolfram. 'Bringing Home the Bacon', *Art and Artists*, Nov. 1971, pp. 42–5 (illus.).

Charles Spencer. 'Non sono mai riscuto a dipingere un sorriso', *Bolaffiarte*, Nov. 1971, pp. 45–8 (illus.).

Xavier Gauthier. 'L'homme insulté de Bacon', *La Galerie*, Nov. 1971, p. 68 (illus.).

Claude Bouyeure. 'Francis Bacon ou la réalité piégée', *Jardin des arts*, Nov. 1971, pp. 6–7 (illus.).

Jérôme Peignot. 'Bacon', *Opus International*, 28, Nov. 1971, pp. 44–7, 65–6 (illus.).

Sabine Marchand. 'A la découverte de Francis Bacon', *Le Figaro*, 1 Nov. 1971 (illus.).

Monique Dittière. 'Francis Bacon réinvente la figure humaine', *L'Aurore*, 3 Nov. 1971, p. 12 (illus.).

Michel Conil Lacoste. 'Francis Bacon: le paradoxe du tragique et du suave', *Le Monde*, 3 Nov. 1971, p. 15 (illus.).

Jacques Michel. 'Entretien avec un portraitiste de l'inimaginable', *Le Monde*, 3 Nov. 1971, p. 15.

Andrew Forge. 'Francis Bacon au Grand Palais', *Listener*, 4 Nov. 1971, pp. 630–2 (illus.).

Robert Melville. 'Bacon Agonistes', *New Statesman*, 5 Nov. 1971, p. 627.

Maurice Rheims. 'Les Artifices du délire', *Nouvelles littéraires*, 5 Nov. 1971, pp. 18–19 (illus.).

Sheldon Williams. 'Best Bacon', *Spectator*, 6 Nov. 1971, pp. 641 (cover), 657 (illus.).

André Fermigier. 'Le fauteuil de l'inquisiteur', *Le Nouvel Observateur*, 8 Nov. 1971, pp. 58–9 (illus.).

Frank Elgar. 'Francis Bacon: "le plus important des artistes vivants"', *Carrefour*, 10 Nov. 1971 (illus.).

Georges Bourdaille. 'Francis Bacon: figures en crise', *Lettres françaises*, 10 Nov. 1971, pp. 24–5 (illus.).

Richard Cork. 'Bacon and the Road to Grand Guignol Glory', *Evening Standard*, 11 Nov. 1971, p. 12.

Norbert Lynton. 'Victims of Paint', *Guardian*, 11 Nov. 1971.

'Francis Bacon, l'idole de Londres au Grand Palais', *Politique Hebdo*, 11 Nov. 1971.

Pierre Cabanne. 'Bacon, une dialectique du paroxysme', *Combat*, 15 Nov. 1971 (illus.).

Jeanine Baron. 'Francis Bacon: un univers en marge de la réalité et la beauté', *La Croix*, 15 Nov. 1971 (illus.).

'Est-il méchant?' [interview], *L'Express*, 15–21 Nov. 1971, pp. 98–100 (illus.).

Richard Boston. 'Meat and Poison', *Guardian*, 15 Nov. 1971.

Denys Sutton. 'Bacon in Paris', *Financial Times*, 16 Nov. 1971 (illus.).

Françoise Choay. 'La peinture scandaleuse de Francis Bacon', *Quinzaine littéraire*, 16–30 Nov. 1971, pp. 15–16 (illus.).

'Marguerite Duras s'entretient avec Bacon', *Quinzaine littéraire*, 16–30 Nov. 1971, pp. 16–17 (illus.).

Helene Charliat. 'Bacon, merveilleux et terrifiant', *La Tribune des nations*, 26 Nov. 1971 (illus.).

'Francis Bacon: "les gens ont tendance à être offensés par ce qu'on appelle la vérité"', *Nice matin*, 28 Nov. 1971 (illus.).

Marie-Hélène Camus. 'Francis Bacon', *Humanité-dimanche*, 1 Dec. 1971 (illus.).

Robert Hughes. 'Out of the Black Hole', *Time*, 13 Dec. 1971, p. 66 (illus.).

René-Louis Dumas. 'Au Grand Palais', *Le Cri de la France*, 22 Dec. 1971 (illus.).

Jean Guichard-Meili. 'Francis Bacon: le cauchemar légalisé', *Hebdo, témoignage chrétien*, 23 Dec. 1971.

'Francis Bacon' [interview with Jacques Saraben], *Instants*, Bordeaux, no. 2 (1972), pp. 2–3.

Laurence Guillaume. 'Francis Bacon, une oeuvre de souffrance et de cruauté', *Vision sur les arts*, no. 74 (1972), (illus.).

Camille Bourniquel. 'Devanture des arts: Francis Bacon', *Esprit*, Jan. 1972.

Rolf-Gunter Dienst. 'Francis Bacon', *Das Kunstwerk*, Jan. 1972, pp. 39–40.

Jean Revol. 'Francis Bacon', *Les Lettres nouvelles*, Jan. 1972, pp. 227–31.

Lawrence Gowing. 'Positioning in Representation', *Studio International*, Jan. 1972, pp. 14–22 (illus.).

John Berger. 'The Worst is Not Yet', *New Society*, 6 Jan. 1972, pp. 22–3 (illus.); repr. as 'The Worst is Not Yet Come', in ed. Paul Barker: *Arts in Society*, London: Fontana/Collins, 1977, pp. 66–73; rev. version publ. as 'Francis Bacon and Walt Disney', in Berger: *About Looking*, London: Writers and Readers, 1980, pp. 111–18 (illus.).

Patrick Brogan. 'Francis Bacon Paintings Boost Britain', *The Times*, 11 Jan. 1972, p. 5.

Ellen Schwartz. 'Paris Letter: November', *Art International*, 20 Jan. 1972, pp. 54–8 (ref. pp. 56–7) (illus.).

Eddie Wolfram. 'Francis Bacon, by John Russell', *Art and Artists*, Feb. 1972, pp. 56–7.

Janet Hobhouse. 'Francis Bacon: Retrospective at the Grand Palais', *Arts Magazine*, Feb. 1972, pp. 36–8 (illus.).

Andrew Causey. 'Francis Bacon's European Retrospective', *Illustrated London News*, Feb. 1972, pp. 62–3 (illus.).

William Feaver. 'Shock Treatment', *London Magazine*, Feb.–Mar. 1972, pp. 123–34 (illus.).

'Un exemple de violence dans la peinture contemporaine: Francis Bacon', *Jeunes femmes*, Mar. 1972, pp. 20–1.

Claude Esteban. 'Francis Bacon ou la peinture à vif', *Nouvelle revue française*, Mar. 1972, pp. 32–41.

Derek Southall. 'Bed or Dais', *Studio International*, Mar. 1972, p. 139.

Dr. B. 'Versehrte Körper: Düsseldorfer Bacon-Ausstellung', *Abendzeitung*, Nuremberg, 6 Mar. 1972.

Marie Hullenkremer. 'Wichtigste Schau des Jahres', *Aachener Nachrichten*, 8 Mar. 1972 (illus.).

Gunther Engels. 'Groteskes Gelächter in der Nacht des Grauens: ein entsetzter Visionär', *Bergische Landeszeitung*, Berg-Gladbach, 8 Mar. 1972 (illus.).

Peter Steinhart. 'Der Mensch als Kreisl', *Bergische Morgenpost*, 8 Mar. 1972 (illus.).

Dieter Westecker. 'Der Mensch ist ein Schrei', *Düsseldorfer Nachrichten*, 8 Mar. 1972 (illus.).

Alfred Müller-Gast. 'Bacon geht unter die Haut', *Neue Ruhr-Zeitung*, Essen, 8 Mar. 1972 (illus.).

Karl Diemer. 'Mensch, durch den Fleischwolf gedreht', *Fellbacher Zeitung*, 8 Mar. 1972.

Werner Tamms. 'Besessenheit vom Leben', *Westdeutsche Allgemeine Zeitung*, Essen, 9 Mar. 1972 (illus.).

'The Screaming Limit', *Times Literary Supplement*, 10 Mar. 1972, p. 297.

Wolfgang Richter. 'Der Schrei des geschundenen Menschen', *Aachener Volkszeitung*, 11 Mar. 1972 (illus.).

Herbert Leisegang. 'Der Mensch an erster Stelle', *Lohrer Echo*, 11 Mar. 1972.

H.R. 'Schreie statt Lächeln', *Welt am Sonntag*, Berlin, Hamburg, 12 Mar. 1972 (illus.).

Mathias Schreiber. 'Visionen der Schreckens', *Erlanger Tagblatt*, 13 Mar. 1972 (illus.).

Herbert Leisegang. 'Gelächelt wird nicht: Schreckensbilder von Francis Bacon', *Abendpost-Nachtausgabe*, Frankfurt, 14 Mar. 1972.

'Mittelpunkt ist der deformierte Mensch', *Herforder Kreisblatt*, 15 Mar. 1972 (illus.).

'Tearing the Human Image to Bits – Andrew Forge, Francis Bacon and Michael Levey Talk About Titian' [originally broadcast on BBC Radio 3], *Listener*, 16 Mar. 1972, pp. 334–5 (illus.).

Sabine Schultz. 'Fratzen – zum Davonlaufen!', *Rhein-Neckar-Zeitung*, Heidelberg, 17 Mar. 1972.

Peter Hans Gopfert. 'Kreuzigung als Sinnbild des Menschseins', *Darmstädter Echo*, 21 Mar. 1972 (illus.).

Mathias Schreiber. 'Wir sind potentielles Schlachtfleisch', *Frankfurter Neue Presse*, 21 Mar. 1972 (illus.).

E.E. 'Francis Bacon: Bilder der leidenden Kreatur', *Ruhr-Nachrichten*, Dortmund, 21 Mar. 1972 (illus.).

Wolf Schon. 'Frankenstein im Salon', *Deutsche Zeitung, Christ und Welt*, Stuttgart, 24 Mar. 1972 (illus.).

Wolfgang Stauch-von Quitzow. 'Das Menschenbild als aesthetisches Grauen', *Lübecker Nachrichten*, 24 Mar. 1972.

Klaus Lamza. 'Das zerstörte Menschenleben', *Buerische Zeitung*, Gelsenkirchen-Buer, 30 Mar. 1972 (illus.).

Ronald Alley. 'Bacon X-Rayed' [letter in response to article by Lawrence Gowing, Jan. 1972], *Studio International*, Apr. 1972, p. 144.

Hans P. Schnepel. 'Zurück zum Menschen', *Vorwärts*, Bonn-Bad Godesberg, 6 Apr. 1972 (illus.).

Rudolf Lange. 'Was unter der Oberfläche geschieht', *Hannoverische Allgemeine Zeitung*, 7 Apr. 1972 (illus.).

H.P.R. 'Die Realität des Jetzt', *VDI Nachrichten*, Düsseldorf, 12 Apr. 1972 (illus.).

'Bilder der Angst', *Westfalen-Blatt*, Bielefeld, 13 Apr. 1972.

Hanno Reuther. 'Wie schön ist der Schrei: nochmalige Beschäftigung mit Francis Bacon', *Frankfurter Rundschau*, 15 Apr. 1972 (illus.).

Hermann Dannecker. 'Der Realismus des Schlachthauses', *Saarbrücker Landeszeitung*, 24 Apr. 1972 (illus.).

A. Brinkmann. 'Horror ohne Schock', *Bayern-Kurier*, Munich, 29 Apr. 1972 (illus.).

Cesare Musatti. 'L'aggressività non integrita di un bimbo di due anni', *Bolaffiarte*, May 1972, pp. 46–9 (illus.).

Gerald Schurr. 'Art Dispatch from Europe', *Connoisseur*, May 1972, p. 66.

HJM. *Panthéon*, May 1972, pp. 233–4 (illus.).

Michael Sammler. 'Gegen Inhumanität: Bilder von Francis Bacon – Kompromisslos und Aktuell', *Deutsche Volkszeitung*, Düsseldorf, 11 May 1972 (illus.).

Petra Kipphoff. 'Angst und Einsamkeit', *Gmundner Tagespost*, Schwäbisch Gmund, 27 May 1972.

Yvon Taillandier. 'Francis Bacon ou l'espace du "naissant"', *XXe siècle*, June 1972, pp. 56–66 (illus.).

T. Sakai. ['Visitor at Night: A Confession by Francis Bacon']. *Mizue*, Tokyo, July 1972, pp. 7–41 (illus.).

Marina Vaizey. 'Francis Bacon, by John Russell', *Arts Review*, 15 July 1972, p. 438.

Lucian Freud, Francis Bacon. 'Turner at the Academy' [letter to the Editor], *The Times*, 26 Sept. 1974, p. 15.

Hugh M. Davies. 'Bacon's "Black" Triptychs', *Art in America*, Mar.–Apr. 1975, cover and pp. 62–8 (illus.).

Michel Peppiatt. 'Francis Bacon: The Last Seven Years', *Art Spectrum*, Mar. 1975, pp. 16–21 (illus.).

Susan Sontag. 'Francis Bacon: "About Being in Pain"', *Vogue*, New York, Mar. 1975, pp. 136–7 (illus.).

Anthony Bailey. 'Francis Bacon – "I Wanted to Paint the Scream"', *New York Times*, 16 Mar. 1975, section 2, pp. 1, 34 (illus.).

Grace Glueck. 'Bacon Speaks About Pain and Painting', *New York Times*, 20 Mar. 1975, p. 46

John Russell. 'Art of a New Francis Bacon Is at Met', *New York Times*, 20 Mar. 1975, p. 46 (illus.).

Stephen Spender. 'Armature and Alchemy', *Times Literary Supplement*, 21 Mar. 1975, pp. 290–1 (illus.).

Paul Richard. 'Francis Bacon and His Art: Mirrors of a Horrific Life', *Washington Post*, 21 Mar. 1975, pp. B1, B7 (illus.).

David Sylvester. 'Francis Bacon: A Kind of Grandeur' [incl. excerpt from interview repr. from Sylvester], *Sunday Times Magazine*, 23 Mar. 1975, pp. 22–7, 29–30, 32 (illus.).

Arthur Spiegelman. 'Soft Words from a Painter of Screams', *Vancouver Sun*, 26 Mar. 1975 (illus.).

Hilton Kramer. 'Signs of a New Conservatism in Taste', *New York Times*, 30 Mar. 1975, section 2, p. 31 (illus.).

John Russell. 'Master Class', *Sunday Times*, 30 Mar. 1975.

Douglas Davis. 'Swatches of Bacon', *Newsweek*, 31 Mar. 1975, p. 49 (illus.).

David Sylvester. 'Francis Bacon: Triptych/Figure' [excerpts of interviews from Sylvester], *Arts Magazine*, Apr. 1975, pp. 60–1 (illus.).

Jacob-Baal Teshuva. 'Bacon' [incl. extracts from interview with Peter Beard], *Galerie-jardin des arts*, Apr. 1975, pp. 70, 72–4 (illus.).

Michel Peppiatt. 'Francis Bacon au Metropolitan Museum de New-York', *Le Monde*, 3 Apr. 1975 (illus.).

Nigel Gosling. 'Bacon Talking', *Observer*, 6 Apr. 1975.

Robert Hughes. 'Screams in Paint', *Time*, 7 Apr. 1975, pp. 54–7 (illus.).

Alfred Frankenstein. 'The Tortured Figures of Francis Bacon', *San Francisco Examiner & Chronicle*, 20 Apr. 1975 (illus.).

Thomas B. Hess. 'Blood, Sweat, and Smears', *New York*, 21 Apr. 1975, pp. 94–5 (illus.).

Michael Peppiatt. 'Francis Bacon's Recent Paintings', *Financial Times*, 26 Apr. 1975, p. 8.

David Sylvester. 'The Exhilarated Despair of Francis Bacon' [extract of interview from Sylvester], *Art News*, May 1975, pp. 26–31 (illus.).

Gerrit Henry. 'Bacon is Nowhere Near the Gentleman that Some of Our Rebels Have Made Him Out to Be', *Art News*, May 1975, pp. 31–2 (illus.).

Keith Roberts. 'The Artist Speaks?', *Burlington Magazine*, May 1975, pp. 301–2.

Alan G. Artner. 'Anguish Comes into Vogue in Bacon's Theater of Cruelty', *Chicago Tribune*, 4 May 1975 (illus.).

Harold Rosenberg. 'Aesthetics of Mutilation', *New Yorker*, 12 May 1975, pp. 122–3, 125–6.

William Feaver. 'All Flesh is Meat', *Listener*, 15 May 1975, pp. 652–3 (illus.).

Matthew Lewin. 'Bacon Beliefs', *Hampstead and Highgate Express*, London, 20 May 1975.

'Francis Bacon in der Galerie Marlborough', *Zürchsee-Zeitung*, Stafa, 24 May 1975.

Donald Kuspit. 'Francis Bacon: The Authority of Flesh', *Artforum*, Summer 1975, pp. 50–9 (illus.).

Konstantin Bazarov. 'Interviews with Francis Bacon, by David Sylvester', *Art and Artists*, June 1975, pp. 26–31 (illus.).

Norman W. Canedy. 'Francis Bacon at the Metropolitan Museum', *Burlington Magazine*, June 1975, pp. 425–6, 428 (illus.).

Peter Fuller. 'Interviews with Francis Bacon', *Connoisseur*, June 1975, p. 166.

Carter Ratcliff. 'New York Letter', *Art International*, 15 June 1975, pp. 36–42 (illus.).

Anita Wildmann. 'Francis Bacon', *Luzerner Tagblatt*, 19 June 1975 (illus.).

Helen Lessore. 'Francis Bacon', *Goya*, July–Aug. 1975, pp. 27–33 (illus.).

Jane Holtz Kay. 'A Painter Whose Source is Film', *Christian Science Monitor*, 1 Aug. 1975 (illus.).

'Wenn Kunst zum Schrecken wird . . .', *Schweizerische Handels-Zeitung*, Zürich, 7 Aug. 1975.

Lorenza Trucchi. 'Bacon al Metropolitan di New

York', *Qui Arte Contemporanea*, Sept. 1975, pp. 66–7 (illus.).

Judy Marle. 'The Life and Art of Francis Bacon', *TV Times*, London, 29 Nov.–5 Dec. 1975, pp. 35, 38 (illus.).

Louis le Broquy. 'The Mystery of Fact', *Introspect*, Dublin, No. 1 (Dec. 1975), pp. 12–13 (illus.).

Gilbert Lascault. 'Francis Bacon: les chefs-d'oeuvres reconnus', *XXe siècle*, Dec. 1975, pp. 20–7 (illus.).

Hans Keller. 'The Game Without Rules', *Spectator*, 3 Apr. 1976, pp. 26–7.

Georges Charensol. 'Francis Bacon par David Sylvester', *Les Nouvelles littéraires*, 10 June 1976, p. 25.

'Le No. 1 de l'art d'aujourd'hui: Bacon expose au Musée Cantini à Marseille', *Galerie-jardin des arts*, July–Aug. 1976, pp. 42–7 (illus.).

'Francis Bacon: l'art de l'impossible', *L'Oeil*, July–Aug. 1976, p. 55 (illus.).

Camille Rouvier. '"Entretiens avec Francis Bacon": une introduction à l'exposition inaugurée demain au musée Cantini', *Le Provençal*, Marseille, 8 July 1976, p. 6 (illus.).

Camille Rouvier. 'Un des peintres les plus célébrés de son temps: Francis Bacon au Musée Cantini; une foule considérable à l'inauguration de l'exposition', *Le Provençal*, Marseille, 10 July 1976 (illus.).

Jean-Jacques Levêque. 'Oil on Bacon', *Quotidien du médecin*, Paris, 16 July 1976 (illus.).

F.E. 'Francis Bacon au musée Cantini à Marseille', *Carrefour*, 22 July 1976 (illus.).

Jean-Jacques Levêque. 'Francis Bacon à Marseille: nous sommes tous des voyeurs', *Les Nouvelles littéraires*, 22 July 1976 (illus.).

Jean-Marie Tasset. 'Francis Bacon: grandeur et solitude', *Le Figaro*, 27 July 1976 (illus.).

Jean-Jacques Levêque. 'A Marseilles Bacon: la mort aux trousses', *Quotidien de Paris*, 31 July 1976.

John A. Walker. 'The Van Gogh Industry', *Art and Artists*, Aug. 1976, pp. 4–7.

'Bacon exposé au musée Cantini à Marseille', *Galerie-jardin des arts*, Aug. 1976, pp. 43–9 (illus.).

France Huser. 'Un univers de désesperance', *Le Nouvel Observateur*, 2 Aug. 1976, p. 52 (illus.).

Jacques Michel. 'Les métaphores de Francis Bacon', *Le Monde*, 6 Aug. 1976, pp. 12–13.

Gaetan Picon. 'Francis Bacon: le choc', *Le Point*, 9 Aug. 1976 (illus.).

Frank Elgar. '"Un desespoir joyeux": Francis Bacon au Musée Cantini à Marseille', *Carrefour*, 19 Aug. 1976, p. 11 (illus.).

Y. Nahara. ['Francis Bacon, A Confined Human'], *Mizue*, Tokyo, Sept. 1976, pp. 10–21 (illus.).

P.A. 'Une recherche audacieuse': Francis Bacon', *La Presse française*, 3 Sept. 1976.

Ian Jeffrey. 'Francis Bacon by Lorenza Trucchi', *Arts Review*, 17 Sept. 1976, p. 493.

Anatole Broyard. 'Francis Bacon', *International Herald Tribune*, Paris, 17 Sept. 1976.

Franz Schulze. 'Bacon's Burden', *Art News*, Nov. 1976, pp. 130, 132.

Edmond Jabes. 'Les métamorphoses de Bacon', *Les Nouvelles littéraires*, 20–7 Jan. 1977 (illus.).

Carter S. Wiseman, Edward Behr, Patricia W. Mooney. 'Agony and the Artist' [incl. interview with Edward Behr, 'I only paint for myself'], *Newsweek*, 24 Jan. 1977, pp. 46–9 (illus.).

Michel Leiris. 'Figures de haute tension: une nouvelle exposition Francis Bacon à Paris', *L'Humanité*, 25 Jan. 1977 (illus.).

'Francis Bacon: "la vie n'a pas de sens"', *L'Oeil*, Feb. 1977 (illus.).

O.H. 'Francis Bacon et la joie' [incl. interview with Madeleine Chapsal], *L'Express*, 7–13 Feb. 1977, pp. 10–13 (illus.).

Marina Vaizey. 'A Terrible Beauty', *Sunday Times*, 13 Feb. 1977, p. 39.

Frank Elgar. 'Oeuvres récentes de Francis Bacon: "peindre le cri plus que l'horreur"', *Carrefour*, 17 Feb. 1977 (illus.).

René Micha. 'L'imaginaire de Bacon', *Art International*, Mar.–Apr. 1977, pp. 51–2 (illus.).

Antonio Bonet Correa. 'La estructura coherente de Francis Bacon', *El País*, Madrid, 13 Mar. 1977 (illus.).

Michel Leiris. 'The Art of Francis Bacon' [previously publ., as 'Le grand jeu de Francis Bacon', introd. to

catalogue of Paris, Galerie Claude Bernard, exhib.]. *Times Literary Supplement*, 18 Mar. 1977, p. 309.

Alfred Werner. 'An Expressionistic Englishman', *American Artist*, July 1977, pp. 94–6.

Geraldine Norman. 'Collecting: Signature Tune', *The Times Saturday Review*, 9 July 1977, p. 11 (illus.).

Edward Lucie-Smith. 'Bacon's Contempt', *Evening Standard*, 5 Jan. 1978 (illus.).

John McEwen. 'Convulsive', *Spectator*, 7 Jan. 1978, pp. 23–4.

Antonio Bonet Correa. '"Revulsivo e insolito Bacon"' [repr. of introd. to catalogue of Fundacion Juan March, Madrid, exh., Apr.–May 1978], *Boletin Informativo, Fundacion Juan March*, 71 (May 1978), pp. 33–5 (illus.).

Ernesto Gonzalez Bermejo. '"El optimismo es una forma de imbecilidad": entrevista con Francis Bacon', *Cuadernos para el Dialogo*, Madrid, 8 Apr. 1978, pp. 51–3 (illus.).

Juan Manuel Bonet. 'Francis Bacon: el arte como obsesion', *La Calle*, Madrid, 11–18 Apr. 1978, pp. 52–3 (illus.).

'Tremendo y destructivo da Francis Bacon: conferencia de Antonio Bonet Correa', *El Pais*, Madrid, 15 Apr. 1978 (illus.).

'Bacon' [issue devoted to Bacon], *Opus International*, 68, Summer 1978. Contents: p. 10 Jean-Luc Chalumeau: 'Pourquoi Bacon?'; p. 12 Max Clarac-Serou: 'Les "personnages" de Bacon'; pp. 13–15 Dominique Le Buhan: 'La chair des visages de Francis Bacon'; pp. 16–17 Jean-Luc Chalumeau: 'Sur les Crucifixions'; pp. 18–20 Jean-Louis Pradel: 'Velasquez-Bacon'; pp. 20–2 Gérard-Georges Lemaire: 'L'entrée en matière'; pp. 23–4 Giovanni Joppolo: 'Fortune de Francis Bacon'; pp. 25–7 Michel Gérard: 'L'espace du cri'; pp. 28–31 'Entretien entre René Major et Anne Tronche'; pp. 32–4 Eddy Batache: 'Francis Bacon, ou Les ultimes convulsions de l'humanisme'; pp. 34–42 Reportage: 'Bacon dans son atelier, par Jesse Fernandez' [photographs]; pp. 43–7 Debat: 'A propos de Bacon, avec Byzantios, Franta, Le Boul'c, Parré et Peverelli'; pp. 48–9 'Bacon, lors de son exposition chez Claude Bernard en 1977, photographie par Michel Soskine' [photographs], (illus.).

Udo Kultermann. 'Van Gogh in Contemporary Art', *Voices/South*, Nov.–Dec. 1978, pp. 51–5 (illus.).

Jeanne Silverthorne. *Artforum*, Oct. 1980, pp. 81–4 (illus.).

Geordie Greig. 'Bacon: Still Honing the Razor's Edge', *Now!*, 10–16 Oct. 1980, p. 78 (illus.).

'An Interview with Francis Bacon' [interview with David Sylvester; repr. from Sylvester], *Times Literary Supplement*, 21 Nov. 1980, p. 1318 (illus.).

Miriam Gross. 'Bringing Home Bacon' [interview], *Observer Review*, 30 Nov. 1980, pp. 29–31 (illus.).

Michael Peppiatt. 'Francis Bacon and the Waste Land', *Connaissance des Arts*, 16, May 1981, pp. 40–9; 'Les rêves décomposés de Francis Bacon', pp. 48–57 (illus.).

Michel Leiris. 'Bacon le hors-la-loi', *Critique*, May 1981, pp. 519–25.

John Russell Taylor. 'Bacon's New Creativity', *The Times*, 31 Aug. 1981, p. 5.

Joshua Gilder. 'The S R Interview: "I Think About Death Every Day"', *Saturday Review*, New York, Sept. 1981, pp. 36–9 (illus.); republ. in *Flash Art*, 112, May 1983, pp. 17–21 (illus.).

Catherine Clement. 'Logique de la sensation par Gilles Deleuze: le philosophe absorbé par la peinture', *Le Matin*, 1 Dec. 1981, p. 25 (illus.).

Alain Poirson. 'Une peinture de l'hystérie', *Révolution*, 8 Jan. 1982, pp. 44–5 (illus.).

Jean-Pierre Leonardini. 'Le regard touche la viande: Gilles Deleuze devant Francis Bacon', *L'Humanité*, 22 Apr. 1982 (illus.).

Philippe Murray. 'Les cadavres dans le triptyche: Francis Bacon', *Art Press International*, 59 (May 1982), pp. 15, 19–20 (illus.).

René Micha. 'Le Francis Bacon de Gilles Deleuze', *Art International*, May–June 1982, pp. 109–16 (illus.).

Colin Gordon. 'Pure Presences', *Times Literary Supplement*, 14 May 1982, p. 542.

'(Francis Bacon's Market)', *Artnewsletter*, New York, 2

Nov. 1982, pp. 5–6.

Rolf Laessoe. 'Francis Bacon and T.S. Eliot', *Hafnia: Copenhagen Papers in the History of Art*, no. 9 (1983), pp. 113–30 (illus.).

Gilles Deleuze. 'Francis Bacon, The Logic of Sensation', *Flash Art* 112, May 1983, pp. 8–16 (illus.).

'I Think About Death Every Day' [interview with Joshua Gilder, previously publ. in *Saturday Review*, Sept. 1981], *Flash Art*, 112, May 1983, pp. 17–21 (illus.).

Peter Lennon. 'A Brush with Ebullient Despair – The Times Profile: Francis Bacon', *The Times*, 15 Sept. 1983, p. 8 (illus.).

Marina Vaizey. 'Following Signs at New Art's Crossroads', *Sunday Times*, 18 Sept. 1983, p. 39 (illus.).

John Russell Taylor. 'The Thoughtful Process of Falling off a Log', *The Times*, 20 Sept. 1983, p. 13.

Henry Porter. 'Sides of Bacon', *Sunday Times*, 25 Sept. 1983, p. 35 (illus.).

Peter Fuller. 'The Sleep of Reason', *New Society*, 6 Oct. 1983, pp. 17–18 (illus.); repr. in Fuller: *Images of God*, London: Chatto and Windus, 1985.

Gaia Servadio. 'Gli ultimi fantasmi de Bacon: novità a Londra, in una delle sue rare mostre personali', *La Stampa*, 11 Oct. 1983 (illus.).

Mel Gooding. 'Francis Bacon: Full Face and in Profile', *Arts Review*, 25 Nov. 1983.

Geneviève Breerette. 'Francis Bacon vu par Michel Leiris', *Le Monde*, 7 Dec. 1983, p. 22.

Lawrence Gowing. *Sunday Telegraph*, 11 Dec. 1983, p. 14.

William Packer. 'All on Canvas', *Financial Times*, 17 Dec. 1983, p. 10.

Gilles Deleuze. 'Books', *Artforum*, Jan. 1984, pp. 68–9 (illus.).

'Francis Bacon' [issue publ. on occasion of Galerie Maeght Lelong, Paris, exh., Jan.–Feb. 1984; introd. by Jacques Dupin, interview with David Sylvester], *Repères: Cahiers d'art contemporain*, 10 [Jan. 1984], 36p (illus.).

Michael Gibson. 'Bacon's Grim Sensuality', *International Herald Tribune*, Paris, 28–9 Jan. 1984, p. 4 (illus.).

Alice Bellony-Rewald. 'Entretien: Francis Bacon', *Beaux Arts Magazine*, Feb. 1984, pp. 28–33 (illus.).

Pierre Daix. 'Bacon: le tragique et la peinture', *Le Quotidien de Paris*, 2 Feb. 1984, p. 31 (illus.).

France Huser. 'Falstaff 1984: un entretien avec Francis Bacon', *Le Nouvel Observateur*, 3 Feb. 1984 (illus.).

Patricia de Beauvais. 'Bacon: l'enchanteur écorché', *Paris-Match*, 3 Feb. 1984, pp. 90–3 (illus.).

Peter Campbell. 'Francis and Vanessa', *London Review of Books*, 15 Mar.–4 Apr. 1984, pp. 15–17.

Lorenza Trucchi. 'Ritratto d'artista oltre lo specchio: esce i Italia una grande monografia su Francis Bacon con testo di Michel Leiris', *Il Giornale Nuovo*, 16 Mar. 1984 (illus.).

'Francis Bacon, Michel Leiris', *Art Line*, Apr. 1984 (illus.).

Peter Fuller. 'Francis Bacon: Ludic Hope', *Vanguard*, Vancouver Art Gallery, Apr. 1984, pp. 10–14 (illus.).

John Russell. 'Art: Recent Paintings by Francis Bacon', *New York Times*, 14 May 1984 (illus.).

Michael Peppiatt. 'Francis Bacon: The Studio as Symbol', *Connoisseur*, Sept. 1984, cover and pp. 84–93 (illus.).

5. Films

Francis Bacon: Paintings 1944–1962. Samaritan Films (London) for Arts Council and Marlborough Fine Art; dir./scr. David Thompson, 1963.

Francis Bacon. Alexandre Burger for Radio Télévision Suisse Romande; dir. Pierre Koralnik, 1964.

Sunday Night Francis Bacon: Interviews with David Sylvester. BBC Television; dir. Michael Gill, 1966.

Francis Bacon. ORTF; dir. J.M. Berzosa; interview with Maurice Chapuis, 1971.

Francis Bacon, Grand Palais 1971. BBC Television, prod. by Colin Nears; dir. by and interview with Gavin Millar, 1971.

Sides of Bacon. London Weekend Television for *Aquarius*; prod. Derek Bailey, dir. Bruce Gowers;

incl. interview with David Sylvester; screened 29 Nov. 1975 (provinces), 30 Nov. 1975 (London).

Fenêtre sur . . . Peintres de notre temps: Francis Bacon. Antenne 2; prod. Michel Lancelet, dir. Georges Paumier; interview with Michel Lancelet and Edward Behr; screened 19 Apr. 1977.

Après Hiroshima . . . Francis Bacon. Antenne 2 for *Désirs des arts*, presented by Pierre Daix; dir. Pierre-Andre Boutang, P. Collin; interview with Pierre Daix; screened 5 Feb. 1984.

The Brutality of Fact, BBC Television for *Arena*; dir. Michael Blackwood; prod. Alan Yentob; interview with David Sylvester; screened 16 Nov. 1984 (London).

6. One-man Exhibition Catalogues

[? 1929]. London, 7 Queensberry Mews West, SW7 [exh. of furniture and rugs]. [No catalogue].

1934, Feb. London, Transition Gallery [Sunderland House, Curzon Street W1]. [No catalogue].

1951, Dec.–Feb. 1952. London, Hanover Gallery. [No catalogue].

1952, Dec.–Jan. 1953. London, Hanover Gallery. [No catalogue].

1953, Nov.–Dec. London, Beaux-Arts Gallery. [No catalogue].

1953, Oct.–Nov. New York, Durlacher Bros. (13 works).

1954, June–July. London, Hanover Gallery. [No catalogue].

[1955, Jan.–Feb.]. London, ICA (13 works). Introd. by Max Clarac-Serou.

1957, Feb.–Mar. Paris, Rive Droite. (21 works). Introd. by Roland Penrose, David Sylvester.

1957, Mar.–Apr. London, Hanover Gallery. (15 works).

1958, Jan.–Feb. Turin, Galleria Galatea. (8 works). Introd. by Luigi Carluccio.

1958, Feb.–Mar. Milan, Galleria dell'Ariete. (9 works). Introd. by David Sylvester, Toni del Renzio.

1958, Mar. Rome, L'Obelisco. (8 works). Introd. by Toni del Renzio.

1959, June–July. London, Hanover Gallery. (10 works).

1959, July–Aug. Chicago, Richard L. Feigen. (12 works).

1960, Mar.–Apr. London, Marlborough Fine Art. (32 works). Introd. by Robert Melville.

1961, Feb.–Mar. Nottingham, University, Dept. of Fine Art. (34 works). Introd. by Helen Lessore.

1962, May–July. London, Tate Gallery. (91 works). Introd. by John Rothenstein, text by Ronald Alley.

1962, Sept.–Oct. Turin, Galleria Civica d'Arte Moderna. (83 works). Introd. by Luigi Carluccio.

1962, Oct.–Nov. Milan, Galleria d'Arte Galatea. (10 works). Introd. by Luigi Carluccio.

1962, Oct.–Nov. Zürich, Kunsthaus. (78 works). Introd. by Sir John Rothenstein, Stephen Spender.

1963, Feb. Amsterdam, Stedelijk Museum. (73 works). Introd. by Stephen Spender.

1963, July–Aug. London, Marlborough Fine Art (New London Gallery). (13 works). Interview with David Sylvester.

1963, Oct.–Nov. New York, Granville Gallery.

1963, Oct.–Jan. 1964. New York, Solomon R. Guggenheim Museum. (65 works). Introd. by Lawrence Alloway. Travelling to Chicago, Art Institute.

1964, Sept.–Nov. Houston, Contemporary Arts Associates. (15 works).

1965, Jan.–Feb. Hamburg, Kunstverein. (61 works). Introd. by Ronald Alley.

1965, Feb.–Apr. Stockholm, Moderna Museet. (63 works). Introd. by Ronald Alley.

1965, Apr.–May. Dublin, Municipal Gallery of Modern Art. (57 works).

1965, July–Aug. London, Marlborough New London Gallery. (9 works). Introd. by John Russell.

1966, Jan.–Feb. Milan, Toninelli Arte Moderna. (11 works). Introd. by Luigi Carluccio.

1967, Mar.–Apr. London, Marlborough New London Gallery. (20 works). Introd. by Michel Leiris; interview with David Sylvester.

1967, June–July. Siegen, Oberes Schloss. (8 works). Introd. by Carl Linfert, Michel Leiris, Arnold Bode.

1968, Nov.–Dec. New York, Marlborough-Gerson Gallery. (20 works). Introd. by Lawrence Gowing.

1970, Mar.–Apr. Turin, Galleria Galatea. (9 works). Introd. by Tommaso Chiaretti.

1971, Oct.–Jan. 1972. Paris, Grand Palais. (108 works). Introd. by Michel Leiris; travelling to Düsseldorf, Städtische Kunsthalle (Mar.–May 1972).

1972, Dec.–Jan. 1973. Milan, Galleria del Milione. (12 works). Introd. by Gianfranco Bruno.

1975, Mar.–June. New York, Metropolitan Museum of Art. (36 works). Introd. by Henry Geldzahler; interview with Peter Beard.

1976, July–Sept. Marseilles, Musée Cantini. (16 works). Introd. by Gaetan Picon.

1977, Jan.–Mar. Paris, Galerie Claude Bernard. (20 works). Introd. by Michel Leiris.

1977, Oct.–Dec. Mexico, Museo de Arte Moderno. (13 works). Introd. by Juan Acha, Michel Leiris.

1978, Feb. Caracas, Museo de Arte Contemporaneo. (12 works). Introd. by Michel Leiris.

1978, Apr.–May. Madrid, Fundacion Juan March. (17 works). Introd. by Antonio Bonet Correa; travelling to Barcelona, Fundacio Joan Miró (June–July 1978).

1980, Mar.–May. Mannheim, Städtische Kunsthalle. Text by Joachim Heusinger von Waldegg.

1980, Apr.–June. New York, Marlborough Gallery. (13 works).

1983, June–Aug. Tokyo, National Museum of Modern Art. (45 works). Essay by Masanori Ichikawa; introd. by Sir Lawrence Gowing; travelling to Kyoto (National Museum of Modern Art, Sept.–Oct. 1983) and Nagoya (Aichi Prefectural Art Gallery, Nov. 1983).

1984, [Jan.–Feb.]. Paris, Galerie Maeght Lelong. (16 works). Introd. by Jacques Dupin; interview with David Sylvester.

1984, May–June. New York, Marlborough Gallery. (11 works).

[1984, June]. London, Thomas Gibson. (3 works). Introd. by David Sylvester.

7. Group Exhibition Catalogues

[? 1930]. London, 7 Queensberry Mews West, SW7 [joint exh. with Roy de Maistre]. [No catalogue traced].

1933, Apr. London, Mayor Gallery. *Exhibition of Recent Paintings by English, French and German Artists*. (1 work).

1933, Oct. London, Mayor Gallery. [Exh. of works selected by Herbert Read to mark the publication of his book *Art Now*]. (1 work).

[1937, Jan.]. London, Thomas Agnew. *An Exhibition of Paintings*. (4 works).

1945, Apr. London, Lefevre Gallery. *Recent Paintings by Francis Bacon, Frances Hodgkins, Henry Moore, Matthew Smith, Graham Sutherland*. (2 works).

1946, Feb. London, Lefevre Gallery. *Recent Paintings by Ben Nicholson, Graham Sutherland, and Francis Bacon, Robert Colquhoun, John Craxton, Lucian Freud, Robert MacBryde, Julian Trevelyan*. (2 works).

1946, July–Aug. London, Lefevre Gallery. *British Painters Past and Present*. (1 work).

1946, Sept.–Oct. London, Tate Gallery. *The Contemporary Art Society*. (1 work).

1949, Nov.–Dec. London, Hanover Gallery. *Francis Bacon: Paintings; Robin Ironside: Coloured Drawings*. (12 works).

1950, Mar.–Apr. London, ICA. *London/Paris: New Trends in Painting and Sculpture*. (3 works).

1950, Sept.–Oct. London, Hanover Gallery. *Posters; Francis Bacon: Recent Paintings; Hilly: Paintings*.

1950, Oct.–Dec. Pittsburgh, Carnegie Institute. *The Pittsburgh International Exhibition of Paintings*. (1 work).

1950, Dec.–Jan. 1951. Leeds, City Art Gallery. *Fifteen Contemporary British Painters*. (5 works).

1951. London, Arts Council. *British Painting 1925–1950: First Anthology* [organized for Festival of Britain]. (3 works).

1952, July–Aug. London, ICA. *Recent Trends in Realist Painting.* (2 works).

1953, Mar.–Apr. London, ICA. *Wonder and Horror of the Human Head: An Anthology.* (1 work).

1954, June–Oct. Venice. *XVII esposizione biennale internazionale d'arte.* (12 works).

[1954], Oct.–Nov. New York, Martha Jackson Gallery. *3 British Artists: Hepworth, Scott, Bacon.* (4 works).

1955, May–Aug. New York, Museum of Modern Art. *The New Decade: 22 European Painters and Sculptors.* (4 works).

[1955], June–July. London, Hanover Gallery. *Bacon, Scott, Sutherland.* (5 works).

1956, Jan. Palm Beach (Fla.), Society of the Four Arts. *Contemporary British Painting.* (3 works).

1956, May–June. Oslo, Kunstnernes Hus. *Britisk Natidskunst.* (2 works).

1956, Oct.–Nov. New York, E. & A. Silberman Galleries. *An Exhibition of Contemporary British Art.* (1 work).

1956, Oct.–Dec. New York, Museum of Modern Art. *Masters of British Painting 1800–1950.* (6 works).

1957, Oct. Paris, Salle Balzac. *La Peinture britannique contemporaine.* (4 works).

1958, [May–June]. London, Arts Council (in Bath, Victoria Art Gallery). *Three Masters of Modern British Painting: Sir Matthew Smith, Victor Pasmore, Francis Bacon.* (14 works).

1958, July. London, Arthur Tooth. *Critic's Choice: 1958 Selection by David Sylvester.* (4 works).

1958, Sept.–Oct. London, Arts Council (in Leicester, Museum and Art Gallery). *Paintings from the Urvater Collection.* (2 works).

1959, Sept.–Oct. São Paulo, Museu de Arte Moderna. *V bienal.* (12 works).

1959, Sept.–Nov. New York, Museum of Modern Art. *New Images of Man.* (5 works).

1960. Moscow, Pushkin Museum. *Zhivopis' Velikobritanii 1700–1960 [British painting 1700–1960].* (2 works).

1960, Apr.–May. London, Tate Gallery. *Contemporary Art Society.* (3 works).

1960, May. Paris, Musée d'Art Moderne de la Ville de Paris. *XVIe Salon de Mai.* (1 work).

1960, Oct.–Dec. Los Angeles, University of California, Art Galleries. *Francis Bacon, Hyman Bloom.* (10 works).

1961, Feb. New York, Museum of Modern Art. *The James Thrall Soby Collection.* (2 works).

1961, May. Milan, Da Falanga. *Tra l'antico e il moderno.* (2 works).

1962, [Feb.–Mar.]. Lisbon, Fundaçao Calouste Gulbenkian. *Arte britanica no seculo XX.* (5 works).

1962, Apr. Milan, Luca Scacchi Gracco. [Group exh.] (3 works).

1962, Apr.–Oct. Seattle, World's Fair. *American and International Art Since 1950.* (3 works).

1962, Oct.–Dec. Eindhoven, Stedelijk van Abbe-Museum. *Kompas 2: Hedendaagse schilderkunst uit Londen/Contemporary Paintings in London.* (5 works).

1962, Nov.–Dec. San Francisco, Museum of Art. *British Art Today.* (3 works).

1963, Jan.–Feb. Milan, Luca Scacchi Gracco. [Group exh.] (2 works).

[1963], Mar.–Apr. Naples, Galleria il Centro. *Bacon–Sutherland.*

1963, May–June. Paris, Grand Palais. *Art contemporain.* (3 works).

1964, Feb.–Mar. London, ICA. *Study for an Exhibition of Violence in Contemporary Art.* (4 works).

1964, Apr.–June. Bochum, Städtische Kunsthalle. *Profile III: Englische Kunst der Gegenwart.* (5 works).

1964, Apr.–June. London, Tate Gallery. *54–64: Painting and Sculpture of a Decade.* (5 works).

1964, May–July. Düsseldorf, Kunstverein für die Rheinlande und Westfalen. *Britische Malerei der Gegenwart.* (6 works).

1964, July–Oct. Ghent, Museum voor Schone Kunsten. *Figuratie defiguratie de menselijke figuur sedert Picasso.* (6 works).

1964, Sept.–Oct. Humlebaek, Louisiana. *Engelsk maleri i dag.* (4 works).

1965, Nov.–Dec. New York, Marlborough-Gerson Gallery. *The English Eye.* (4 works).

1966, Mar. Irvine (Calif.), Univ. of California, Art Gallery. *Five Europeans: Bacon, Balthus, Dubuffet, Giacometti, Morandi.* (4 works).

1966, [June–July]. Cleveland, Museum of Art. *Fifty Years of Modern Art, 1916–1966.* (2 works).

1966, June–July. Recklinghausen, Städtische Kunsthalle. *Variationen (20. Ruhrfestspiele Recklinghausen).* (5 works).

1966, June–Sept. London, Hanover Gallery. *The Poetic Image.* (2 works).

1966, July–Aug. London, Marlborough Fine Art. *19th and 20th Century Masters.* (2 works).

1967, May–July. Saint-Paul, Fondation Maeght. *Dix ans d'art vivant: 1955–1965.* (3 works).

1967, July–Aug. London, Marlborough Fine Art. *Recent Acquisitions.* (3 works).

1967, Nov.–Dec. Dublin, Royal Dublin Society. *Rosc '67: The Poetry of Vision.* (2 works).

1968, Mar.–May. Hamburg, Kunstverein. *Britische Kunst heute.* (2 works).

1968, Apr.–May. London, ICA. *The Obsessive Image 1960–1968.* (2 works).

1968, Apr.–May. New York, Marlborough-Gerson Gallery. *International Expressionism, Part 1.* (2 works).

1968, July–Aug. London, Marlborough Fine Art. *Recent Acquisitions 1968.* (2 works).

1968, Sept.–Nov. Darmstadt, Kunsthalle. *Menschenbilder.* (2 works).

[1969, May]. London, Marlborough Fine Art (on board *Queen Elizabeth 2*). *A Selection of 20th Century British Art.* (3 works).

1969, June–July. Turin, Galleria Galatea. *Selezione 9.* (2 works).

[1969, Oct.–Jan. 1970]. London, Marlborough Fine Art. *European Masters.* (2 works).

1970, May–July. Recklinghausen, Städtische Kunsthalle. *Zeitgenossen: das Gesicht unserer Gesellschaft im Spiegel der heutigen Kunst (Ruhrfestspiele Recklinghausen 1970.* (3 works).

1971. New York, Marlborough Gallery. *Masters of the 20th Century.* (3 works).

1971, Sept.–Nov. Mechelen, Cultureel Centrum Burgomeester A. Spinoy. *De menselijke figuur in de kunst 1910–1960.* (2 works).

1972, Summer. London, Marlborough Fine Art. *Masters of the 19th and 20th Centuries.* (2 works).

1972, June–July. London, Fischer Fine Art. *A Journey into the Universe of Art, from Courbet and Corot to Bacon, Moore and Lindner.* (4 works).

1972, Nov. London, Arts Council (in Whitechapel Art Gallery). *Decade 40's: Painting, Sculpture and Drawing in Britain 1940–49.* (3 works).

1973, Caracas, Museo de Bellas Artes. *Cuatro maestros contemporaneos: Giacometti, Dubuffet, De Kooning, Bacon.* (11 works). Organized by International Council of the Museum of Modern Art, New York.

1973, Summer. London, Marlborough Fine Art. *Selected European Masters of the 19th and 20th Centuries.* (2 works).

1973, Sept.–Oct. São Paulo, Museu de Arte. *4 mestres contemporanoes: Jean Dubuffet, Alberto Giacometti, Willem de Kooning, Francis Bacon.* (10 works). Travelling to Rio de Janeiro.

1973, Sept.–Nov. Brussels, Palais des Beaux-Arts. *Henry Moore to Gilbert and George: Modern British Art from the Tate Gallery (Europalia 73 Great Britain).* (8 works).

1974, Nov.–Jan. 1975. Milan, Palazzo Reale. *La ricerca dell'identità.* (6 works).

1975, May–June. Turin, Galleria Galatea. *Selezione 12.* (4 works).

1975, Sept.–Nov. Los Angeles, County Museum of Art. *European Painting in the Seventies: New Work by Sixteen Artists.* (2 works).

1975, Oct.–Jan. 1976. Liverpool, Walker Art Gallery. *Peter Moores Liverpool Project 3: Body & Soul.* (5 works).

1976, [Aug.]. London, Arts Council (in Hayward Gallery). *The Human Clay.* (1 work).

1977, Mar.–Apr. Madrid, Galeria Theo. *Francis Bacon, Pablo Picasso.* (6 works).

1977, May–Sept. Bordeaux, Galerie des Beaux-Arts. *La Peinture britannique de Gainsborough à Bacon.* (4 works).

1977, July–Oct. Bregenz, Künstlerhaus. *Englische Kunst der Gegenwart.* (10 works).

1977, Sept.–Nov. London, Royal Academy. *British Painting 1952–1977.* (5 works).

1978, Sept.–Oct. Des Moines, Art Center. *Art in Western Europe: The Postwar Years 1945–1955.* (4 works).

1978, Oct.–Dec. London, Felicity Samuel Gallery. *Clive Barker: 12 Studies of Francis Bacon; Francis Bacon: 3 Studies of Clive Barker.*

1980, May–June. Berlin, Schloss Charlottenburg, Grosse Orangerie. *Zeichen des Glaubens, Geist der Avantgarde: Religiöse Tendenzen in der Kunst des 20. Jahrhunderts.* (3 works).

1981, Jan.–Mar. London, Royal Academy. *A New Spirit in Painting.* (5 works).

1981, Oct.–Jan. 1982. New Haven (Conn.), Yale Center for British Art. *Eight Figurative Painters.* (6 works).

1982, Apr.–July. Amsterdam, Stedelijk Museum. *'60/'80: Attitudes, Concept, Image.* (4 works).

1983, Apr.–May. New York, Marlborough Gallery. *Britain Salutes New York: Paintings and Sculpture by Contemporary Artists.* (4 works).

1983, May–June. New York, Marlborough Gallery. *Masters of the 19th and 20th Centuries.* (2 works).

1983, Oct.–Dec. Basel, Galerie Beyeler. *Expressive Malerei nach Picasso.* (3 works).

1984, June–Aug. Basel, Galerie Beyeler. *Nudes/nus/Nackte.* (2 works).

1984, July–Sept. London, Tate Gallery. *The Hard-won Image: Traditional Method and Subject in Recent British Art.* (2 works).